The PhD Handbook for the Academic Job Search

Also from Anthony & Coghill-Behrends

CV Handbook: A curriculum vitae owner's manual (The best reference on the market for those with a PhD, MFA, MD, DDS, and a whole lotta brains). PhD Books, 2011. www.phdbooks.com

Getting Hired: A Student Teacher's Guide to Professionalism, Résumé Development & Interviewing (2010). Kendall Hunt Publishing. www.kendallhunt.com

Books by R. Anthony and G. Roe

101 Grade A Résumés for Teachers, Barron's, third ed.

The Curriculum Vitae Handbook: How to Present and Promote Your Academic Career, Rudi Publishing, second ed.

From Contact to Contract: A Teacher's Employment Guide, Sulzburger & Graham Publishing, Ltd., second ed.

Over 40 and Looking for Work? A Guide for the Unemployed, Underemployed, and Unhappily Employed, Bob Adams, Inc.

How to Look Good to an Employer, Pearson Education.

Educators' Passport to International Jobs, Peterson's Guides.

Finding a Job in Your Field: A Handbook for Ph.D.'s & M.A.'s, Peterson's Guides.

The PhD Handbook for the Academic Job Search

An owner's manual for finding jobs

The best reference on the market for those with a PhD, MFA, MD, DDS and a whole lotta brains.

Will Coghill-Behrends & Rebecca Anthony

PhD Books, LLC, Publisher

For Inquires about this publication or about the services available through PhD Books, please visit www.phdbooks.com
Find us on Facebook: PhD Books

First Edition, 2012

PRINTED IN THE UNITED STATES OF AMERICA

ISBN-13: 978-1475025903
ISBN-10: 1475025904

Contents

Your PhD Planner 10
Introduction 12

Part 1: The PhD Job Search 14

PhD Planner – Part I (Planners 1-7) 15

Job Search Timeline 16

Doctoral Program Synopsis 18
Job Search Year Synopsis 19
Pre-Search Planning 20

Marketing Your Degree 23

Enrollments in Higher Education 24
Establishing your Marketing Plan 26
Who are you? Teacher-Scholar or Scholar-Teacher? 27
Marketing Budget 28
Understanding Marketing Context 29
Pricing: Your Academic Capital 30

Institutional Fit 32

Institutions Granting Graduate Degrees 33
Institutions Granting Baccalaureates as the Highest Degrees 35
Institutions Granting Associates as the Highest Degrees 35
Non-"PROF" Professional Opportunities 36

Decoding Job Descriptions 38

Sample Faculty Job Announcement 39
Title/Level of Position 40
Term of Appointment 40
Responsibilities and Duties 41
Required or Preferred Qualifications 41
Starting Date 42
Application Deadline 42
Salary 43
Notes 44

Contents

Part 2: Tools of the Trade 46

PhD Planner – Part II (Planners 8-17) 47

The Curriculum Vitae (CV) 48

Contact Information and Education 51
Teaching and Research Experiences 51
Publications, Presentations, Leadership & Service 52
References 53
Inappropriate Material for your CV 54
CV Basics 55
Action Words 57
CV Categories 58
Sample CVs 61
Professional Résumés for Non-faculty Positions 65
Sample Résumé 66

Recommendations & References 67

Letters & Professional References 67
Managing your Letters of Recommendation 68
Myths of Letters of Recommendation 69
Sharing your Letters of Recommendation 73

21st Century Communication 74

Cover Letters 76
Salutation 76
Introduction 77
Body 78
Conclusion 81
Requests for Additional Materials 82
Thank You Letters 83
Accepting & Rejecting Offers 83
Focus your Letter 84
Sample Letter with Key Callouts 86
Sample Cover Letter for Tenure-track Position 87
Sample Cover Letter for Position Outside Academe 89
Sample Thank You Letter 90

Contents

Sample Rejection Letter 91
Sample Job Offer Acceptance Letter 92
Keeping Good Records 93

Philosophy Statements 94
Teaching Philosophy 94
Writing a Research Statement 96
Research & Teaching Agendas 98

Interview Portfolios 101
Portfolio Artifacts 102
Inappropriate ePortfolio Materials 104
Social Media and your ePortfolio 105
Notes 107

Part 3: Interviews, Offers & Negotiations 109

PhD Planner — Part III (Planners 18-25) 110

Interviews: The Art of Selling You 111
Doing Your Homework 112
The Interview 115
Screening Interviews 115
Skype, Web-Conference & Phone Interviews 116
Selection Interviews: The On-Campus Visit 119
Budgeting your On-Campus Visit 120
Knowing your Interview Itinerary 122
Sample On-Campus Interview Itinerary 123
Job Talk & Presentations 125
Teaching Demonstrations 127
Image: Clothing, Body Language & Presence 129
Body language 131
Formal Dining Situations 132

Interview Questions 136
Interview Questions You can Expect 137
50 Common Interview Questions 138
Interview Topics 140

Contents

Inappropriate Questions 141
Questions for the Search Committee 142
Questions about Teaching 142
Questions About Research 143
Questions About Tenure 143
Picking up on Conversational Cues 144
Interview Follow Up: Evaluating your Interview Performance 144

The Offer 146
Elements of an Offer 147
Sample Contract Offer Letter 148
Considering the College 150
Considering your Career 150
Considering the Community 151
Balancing Multiple Offers 152

Negotiations 153
What's Negotiable? 154

Saying Thanks 155
Notes 156

Part 4: Professional Associations 158

Arts & Communication 159
Counseling & Human Services 165
Diversity Resources & Higher Education 169
Education & Student Services 170
Health & Recreation 197
History, Ethnic & Cultural Histories 204
Languages, Literature & Writing 207
Libraries & Museums 211
Mathematics, Technology & Business 213
Philosophy & Religion 218
Sciences 221
Social Sciences 225

Contents

Part 5: PhD Planner 227

PhD Planner Contents 228

Monthly Academic Planner 230
A Four Year Plan 232
Planning for Comprehensive Exams/Thesis Proposals 233
Academic Job Search Budget 234
Inventory of Professional Readiness 235
Institutional Fit Inventory 236
Creating and Using a Support Network 237
Letters of Recommendation 238
Transcripts 240
Marketing Tools 241
Letter and Application Log 242
Teaching Philosophy Inventory 243
Teaching Philosophy Profile 244
Teaching Agenda 245
Research Inventory 246
Research Profile 247
Portfolio Checklist 248
Employer Profile 249
On-Campus Visit 250
Interview Notes 251
Apparel and Packing Planner 252
Community Inventory 253
Academic Negotiations 254
My Thank You List 256
Notes 257

Your PhD Planner

The academic job search is riddled with complicated rituals that can confuse even the brightest of scholars. This book is designed to help you make the most of your academic job search before, during, and at the conclusion of the process. This handbook demystifies the necessities and practices associated with the job search. The book contains wisdom from helping several hundred doctoral and professional students make the jump from student to professor. We are especially excited to include, "The PhD Planner" with tools to help you organize your search tools, your search timeline, and your job search decision-making process. Within the pages of the PhD Planner, you'll find prompts designed to get you thinking about various components of a given topic that even the most astute job-seekers might overlook because of the harried nature of the academic job search. The PhD Planner includes:

1	**Monthly Academic Planner** Because mapping your year is a good idea
2	**A Four Year Plan** Long-term planning for courses
3	**Planning for Comprehensive Exams/Thesis Proposals** The trials and tribulations of a doc student
4	**Academic Job Search Budget** Manage your dough
5	**Inventory of Professional Readiness** Progress check
6	**Institutional Fit Inventory** If the shoe fits...
7	**Creating and Using a Support Network** I get by with a little help from my friends
8	**Letters of Recommendation** Who can speak to my potential as a scholar?
9	**Transcripts** Evidence of degree attainment

10	**Marketing Tools** My scholarly proof
11	**Letter and Application Log** Staying on top of your applications
12	**Teaching Philosophy Inventory** Knowing your stuff as a teacher
13	**Teaching Philosophy Profile** My beliefs on teaching and learning in the academy
14	**Teaching Agenda** In a perfect world, I'd teach...
15	**Research Inventory** Because knowing your research matters
16	**Research Profile** My beliefs on research in my field
17	**Portfolio Checklist** Showcasing my goods
18	**Employer Profile** Advanced interview homework
19	**On-Campus Visit** Advanced interview preparation
20	**Interview Notes** The basic questions you have to nail
21	**Apparel and Packing Planner** Looking good was never this easy
22	**Community Inventory** Can I live here?
23	**Academic Negotiations** There's more to this than salary Part 1
24	**Academic Negotiations** There's more to this than salary Part 2
25	**My Thank You List** A little thanks goes a long way

Introduction

If you have reached the end of your doctoral program and are in the final year of crafting and defending your dissertation, chances are, you're feeling pretty beaten up. You barely feel like putting on jeans anymore, much less having to go through the motions of tying a tie, ironing your dress slacks, and combing your hair. Many of you could use anti-depressants or uppers. The appeal of methamphetamines slowly begins to make sense to you.

A PhD's Guide to The Academic Job Search is here to help. Although the word *PhD* is in the title of the book, it's really designed for all of you earning a terminal degree – for those who need a little lift to make it through the last days and months of your program. It is your friend, a companion that helps you through the ups and downs of your job search. You have enough to worry about. Use this book and save some brain cells. We'll show you new tools of the academic job search including social media to make the most of your networking and branding potential (who knew the network-of-narcissists, Facebook, could help you land a tenure-track job). We'll talk about the process, from grooming, to courting, to first kisses (ok, that was just to make sure you're still awake) well, actually though, entering into an academic job search really isn't that different from entering into a romantic relationship: one where not all the stakes are even or equal. Let's get ready for one hell of a ride through academic adolescence also known as the Academic Job Search.

The Where is Waldo of the Job Search

Have you ever felt like that character in the search-and-find book, *Where's Waldo*, while in your graduate program? You feel hidden among a sea of graduate students, many of whom upstage you because of their brilliance, charisma, and charm. Have you ever thought, "They won't have any problem finding the job…everyone loves them." Both feelings are normal and natural. Now, it's time to turn your attention to you. It's time to stand out. It's time to find Waldo. We know that you'll have many career options along the way, though only a few may be truly appealing. This process is as much about finding out who you are professionally and personally as it is about marketing who you are. Although we believe that an individual can be challenged and fulfilled by more than one career path, we recognize that the essence of any work experience becomes a fundamentally important part of one's life. For most of us, the degree of satisfaction we find in our careers contributes to the success of our personal and social relationships.

Any job search will be influenced, of course, by the availability of positions and the number of competitors for each job opening. Some fields have an almost desperate demand for qualified people; in others, the supply of qualified people far exceeds the demand for their services. Whatever your particular field of study, whatever the amount of competition you face, you can learn to use job-seeking techniques and employment tactics that will increase your chances for success.

While you can't change the numbers, you can change the odds.

A *PhDs Guide to the Academic Job Search* will help you formulate and carry out an orderly and purposeful job search whether you are seeking a competitive internship, a prestigious fellowship, a first job in the academy or a new and better professional position. The resources will help you identify employment possibilities, understand the selection process, control the information that is presented to potential employers, and to feel satisfied that you have done all that you can to conduct a productive job search.

We have worked with hundreds of PhDs, MDs, DDSs, folks with MFAs, MAs and just about every degree in between. We know that this process can be brutal, demoralizing, and confounding, but it is our sincere interest that you find a bit of inspiration and motivation to make your materials the best that they can be. Ninety percent of the job search occurs before the campus visit, yet so many only give ten percent of their effort to putting together materials that promote, highlight, and truly increase their appeal as a new scholar. Candidates that experience success report taking every step of the process seriously: they have their game faces on. Let's go get a job.

Rebecca & Will, Iowa City, Iowa, 2012

The PhD Job Search

PhD Planner

PART 1: THE PhD JOB SEARCH

Part 1 of *The PhD Handbook for the Academic Job Search* focuses on setting the stage for your job-search success. In this section, you'll learn about the academic job-search timeline, enrollment projections, and how to develop your marketing plan. You'll learn about launching your job search, reading the job descriptions, and discovering institutional fit: which kind of institution suits you the best? The following PhD Planner pages will guide your reflection and work toward this end.

1	**Monthly Academic Planner** Because mapping your year is a good idea
2	**A Four Year Plan** Long-term planning for courses
3	**Planning for Comprehensive Exams and Thesis Proposals** The trials and tribulations of a doc student
4	**Academic Job Search Budget** Manage your dough
5	**Inventory of Professional Readiness** Progress check
6	**Institutional Fit Inventory** If the shoe fits...
7	**Creating and Using a Support Network** I get by with a little help from my friends

Job Search Timeline

The academic job search is a lot like dating. Of course we know that dating can mean different things to different people: some people dig one-night stands, others find them absolutely sophomoric. For some, dating is something that's a long drawn-out romantic journey, while others propose by the second date. So what does this have to do with your job search? Well, for starters, you have to decide what kind of date you are. You have to know what your values are in the academic marketplace, and what kind of search you're capable of. Some, like a one-night stand, feel comfortable going into the job search with no planning (or protection); others are deliberate, careful, and like to plan for everything. Some see the academic job search like the process of finding a life-long mate. If you're seeking a tenure-track position, it's actually not completely impossible to draw the parallels between the two processes.

Long before job advertisements even make it to the *Chronicle of Higher Education* or other academic listings, the academic job-search hourglass has been tipped. Ready, Set, Go! Understand that faculty lines, or any academic position for that matter, typically undergo a justification process. Gone are the days when a faculty retirement, particularly of the tenured variety, is inevitably replaced with a new search. Departments are under more scrutiny than ever in today's economic environment to justify the need for new hires and often, to verify that funding, independent of the institution, may be available in a given field. At many colleges and universities, departments may have to go through a year-long vetting process to get permission or funding to advertise a search.

> *"Our provost now requires that departments complete a significant proposal, including: future outlook for the field, non-college based funding streams, vision for excellence at the department, college, university level. It's a big job and by the time we get to actually advertising we've all envisioned that perfect candidate."*
>
> ~Associate Professor, Biology

In some departments, faculty departures are filled in the short term by adjunct or visiting faculty members. Others require that existing faculty step up to the plate to fill in while decisions are made about the future of that particular position. Bottom line: the hiring department has invested considerable time, energy, and even resources in the process of establishing a new tenure-track position. Several faculty-line proposals have been put on hold or stopped altogether because of faculty disagreement, lack of funding, or lack of thorough justification for the position. By the time you see the job a tremendous investment on the part of the faculty and institution has been made. The jobs you're seeing are real, and more importantly, the faculty behind the job description are committed to finding that perfect candidate.

The academic job search is a lengthy one in comparison to those outside of the academy. You've been at this for a while now: several years of coursework, a year devoted to comprehensive exams and writing the beginnings of your dissertation or thesis, and then sometimes in a very long, drawn-out conclusion, your dissertation takes shape. It's in this final stage that most candidates also find themselves in the middle of the academic job search. This is, however, one major mistake that many job seekers make. They simply start too late. By laying the foundation early-on in your academic career, you pave the way for a more productive job search. For this reason, your job search should begin at least a year before you start applying for jobs. Be strategic and start preparing for your search at least 12 months before you plan to enter the market and make application. Take a look at some of the things you should be doing well in advance of your search.

Early Job Search Strategies			
☐	Start looking at job ads in your field	☐	Attend any and all professional meetings
☐	Begin researching potential colleges	☐	Groom your references
☐	Prepare marketing materials (CV, etc.)	☐	Attend job talks on your campus
☐	Share your timeline with everyone	☐	Get published, get out there!
☐	Submit presentation proposals	☐	Get healthy, exercise, be good to yourself

The next two tables provide a closer look at the timeline associated with graduate studies and in particular, the year of the academic job search. You'll find a description of the phase, common items on the to-do list and the tools you'll need to focus your efforts. Getting the competitive edge means differentiating yourself in a tough market.

Doctoral Program Synopsis

Stage	Phase Description	Your To-Do List	Your Tools
Transitioning Year Years 4-5: Professionalization	In the professionalization stage, you'll complete comps and move on to the dissertation. At this stage you should be actively engaging in professional opportunities with the support of your advisor. During this stage, you'll begin to see yourself as a member of a profession. In your final year you will successfully complete and defend your thesis, most frequently while also actively job seeking. Your professional identity becomes paramount and must be marketed.	You will engage in the following activities: • Active networking • Presentations • Submit publications • Dissertation in progress Get the Competitive Edge: • Establish professional social media presence • Build ePortfolio • Active job seeking and networking throughout your field to make connections with folks who can help you. • Get publications accepted or the equivalent in your field.	In the final years of the program you'll develop job-seeking tools that effectively capture your promise and potential as a scholar: • Curriculum Vitae • Dissertation Abstract • ePortfolio • Evidence of grants • Letters of Recommendation • Teaching Philosophy/Agenda • Research Agenda/statement • Social media presence • References • Presentations/Pubs
Years 1-3: Acculturation Process	During the early years of your terminal degree program, you'll engage in coursework and research or teaching assistantships. You'll join a community of doctoral students engaged in the process of becoming part of the academy. This process acculturates you to the demands of the position and the work you'll be engaged in throughout your career. Strive to see this early phase as one that absolutely contributes to your career success. Too many students just go through the motions.	You will engage in the following activities: • Coursework • Assistantships • Writing course papers • Attending conferences • Departmental meetings Get the Competitive Edge: • Join graduate student leadership groups • Join Diversity organizations • Present posters (based on coursework) • Submit presentation proposals • Join a writing group • Get mini grants	You should attend to the following tools that will be useful during the job search. We recommend starting an ePortfolio to archive documentation of scholarly productivity and quality. • Curriculum Vitae • Honors and awards documentation • Writing samples • Teaching/Research Agendas & Statements • Evidence of teaching: -Syllabi -Video demo -Student/Faculty -Evaluations of teaching

Start Here

Job Search Year Synopsis

Period	Phase Description	Your To-Do List	Timing
Screening/Selection/On-Campus Visit/Offer Period	Screening often happens at professional conferences and meetings. Plan to be there. Selection interviews may be conducted at conferences and professional meetings or, as is currently the trend, may occur over some sort of web-based conferencing service: Skype, Polycom, etc. These can occur at any time following the application deadline. On-campus visits are generally 1-3 days in length. Most frequently occurring Nov-March. While it may take a while to receive the offer, the negotiations process is relatively fast-paced.	You've submitted your application materials, now it's time to start preparing for your screening interviews and campus visits: • PhD Planner pages help direct your interview preparation. • Update your ePortfolio to reflect your most recent work. • Research the institutions to which you've applied and discuss their pros/cons with advisors. • Discuss relocation with significant others/family. • Evaluate and plan for moving expenses, cost of living adjustments, changes in lifestyle.	Late Fall through Spring*
Advertising & Application Period	During the early months of the advertising process, several departments will post positions in professional association publications and websites, and on various websites that serve higher education: The Chronicle of Higher Ed, Inside Higher Ed, Higher Ed Jobs, etc. Pay close attention to job announcements and, in particular, deadlines. Continue to screen for newly posted positions. Some institutions post later than others. Develop routines around the process for searching and applying for jobs.	You will engage in the following activities: • Finalize Curriculum Vitae • Prepare cover letters • Discuss applications with faculty advisors • Collect letters of recommendation (consider opening an Interfolio account) • Develop a business card • Prepare one-page conf. CV • Submit application materials before deadline • Maintain file of applications including all documents submitted • Build relationships across discipline using social media	Late Spring through late fall*

Start Here

*While there is definitely a jobs season in higher ed, particularly for faculty positions, it's quite possible that an opening may occur at any time. Job seekers are strongly encouraged to regularly review new postings and announcements.

Pre-Search Planning

Your pre-search plan should include reviewing job ads and descriptions in your field. It's your last chance to notice any trends, and sneak in last minute CV-boosters. Your upcoming job search shouldn't be a secret to anyone, especially key faculty members who can clue you in to vacancies they've heard of or who can introduce you to the chair of an upcoming search at your next conference (wink, wink). It's also time for you to begin grooming your job-search persona, which includes doing a little bit of detective work while you still can. If there are searches in process in your college or on your campus, try to get involved, either by being a graduate student host, or by attending various campus visit/interview functions (the job talk, teaching presentations, lunch with the grad students). Following each candidate's visit, check in with faculty members about their impressions. What do you think went well? Where did they fall short of your expectations? Faculty involved in the actual search may be tight lipped, but typically others may have no problem pointing out all the strengths and flaws of a given candidate. It's great learning in action.

Academic units are committed to hiring the best, most qualified candidate for the department. Early advertising helps them accomplish this. While not all colleges and universities are created equal in terms of budgets or timelines for academic job searches, we are always blown away at what even colleges with smaller budgets are willing to spend for the right person and how quickly some departments move to snag the best possible candidates. Faculty searches are costly, but those costs pale in comparison to the costs of a faculty member of poor quality. Academic units can't take this chance, so early advertising gives them a broader pool of candidates. We'll discuss where to find jobs shortly, let's continue with the timeline for now.

It's not uncommon for us to hear from candidates in the beginning of their job search, "I just found this job – it's written just for me! It's perfect!" Perhaps nothing energizes a job seeker more than finding "the perfect job." It is, indeed, exciting, motivating, and encouraging. This is what we call the job-search honeymoon. Everything seems perfect, and of course, because you've been trained to believe in yourself (and you should) there's no reason why that department wouldn't want to hire you. Then you start to realize: a) all the work that lies ahead; b) are you really going to convince your significant other to move; c) your dissertation adviser expects your prospectus by Monday. Yep, don't forget that most of you will also be in the throes of daily life: your life, your dissertation, your teaching load, your family, even your dogs still need you. Snap out of the *honeymoon mode*, it's time to get to business. But before we rush into the application process, let's continue our discussion of timeline and why it's important for you to pay close attention.

Following the application deadline faculty begin to review the dozens (to hundreds) of applications that they receive. Several campuses have moved to completely online systems for improving the efficiency and organization of such searches, but online or offline, 101 CVs are still 101 CVs. Academics are a meticulous bunch and it takes time to review all those applicants. Once all materials have been examined, the committee will typically move forward with a smaller pool of candidates. The search committee continues to whittle away at this pool until they arrive at their short list. The short-listed candidates will typically all participate in some sort of screening interview at a conference or a phone, Skype or other web-based video-conferencing conversation. Those who make it this far should be proud of themselves.

If you make it past the screening interviews, which most frequently happen late fall even early in the year (MLA, for example typically occurs either just before or just after the New Year) you've almost made it. This is the most critical time in your job search. The invitation to come to campus may leave you little time to prepare and find someone to take over your freshman composition class. It's critical that you strive to be flexible and open to meet the committee's time frame. If you are that stellar person we think you are, you want to get to campus asap, because your charm will win them over in a heartbeat. If you are one of the top candidates in your field, and many of you will be, you could be facing the prospect of multiple invitations (a good problem to have for sure) but one that can quickly degenerate into a scheduling nightmare. Position yourself in advance to be in the most flexible and organized state that you can be. (This is a good semester to not have a teaching assistantship if you can swing it.)

Campus visits are generally brief, but this short trip can seem like an eternity when one considers the pre-trip stress and preparation followed by the post-trip waiting period. The specifics of the on-campus interview follow in a later chapter. Some offers or rejections come quickly, others seem to never arrive (in fact, some rejections never do quite make it, unfortunately). Understand that you are one of likely three to five candidates who will complete the campus visit. That process can take up to a month, depending on schedules. Following the last candidate, search committees typically move pretty rapidly to extend an offer and conduct final reference and background checks. They know the best candidates will disappear quickly. None-the-less, university HR practices, job negotiations and other delays can seem to take forever. Faculty try to wrap up their searches by the end of the Spring term. Nobody likes working in the summer.

So where are you? It's a good question to try to answer. If you are early to the process, you'll have time to deliberately pace yourself and prepare. If you're jumping on a moving train, as many of you will be, that's fine too, just remember to hang on, burn the midnight oil, and get to work. Your degree program was too much work to blow it now.

Marketing your Degree

Your job search requires a fairly comprehensive marketing plan and considerable knowledge of the hiring trends in your particular field. Some of you are entering encouraging markets while others are well aware of the steep competition for each academic job. Before we get too bogged down in discouraging talk of the poor and difficult academic job market, let's focus on a few positives:

- You have more control over your job search than you think!
- You have options out there for you because of the nature of your training and this book can be your coach!

Let's unpack these ideas a little bit for you. The first: the notion of control. You have serious resources at your fingertips to make the most of your academic job search. Not only will this book help you launch a successful career, but don't forget about all of the other resources that can help you: your adviser, your peers and colleagues, your friends and family, your national and regional professional association and organizations, your campus' graduate college or grad student union. Too many doc students get off on the wrong foot by playing into this idea that they are doomed because of the challenges of the job market. Get over it. You know that one day, sooner or later, you'll either be working in your field, or in a related sort of occupation. It's the latter half of this sentence, the doing something else, that speaks to our second point.

Many of you have spent six years convincing yourselves that only tenure-track faculty positions are the kind of job you'll do. Sure, if you have the option, that's wonderful. But what happens, if, in spite of your best efforts, the other candidates get the jobs? What, if, in spite of your best efforts, you don't get any calls for interviews? What happens when next spring you don't have a faculty job? Some give up, curse the academy, and then get bitter. Most are bitter for a little while (it's ok – we should have better prepared you for this reality, or you should have listened when your advisor encouraged you to get more papers submitted). Bottom line: you're intelligent, creative, and can pull this together. There are lots of jobs for folks just like you from corporations to the public sector. Your degree is in demand. You have to know how to market it to different groups. Marketing yourself effectively to various audiences including:

search committees, corporations, non-profits, government agencies, among others, requires serious knowledge of how your qualifications and degree status fit into their needs. Who are you to them? You might feel like you're one of a million others with your same degree and qualifications, but guess what: you are actually part of a very small group of people with terminal degrees. That's pretty special, and frankly not that common. Use it to your advantage. You've got the power.

Here are some facts that just might make you think about the importance of understanding the academic marketplace and the need for you to invest the energy and ego required to develop a comprehensive plan to promote yourself.

Enrollments in Higher Education

Higher education has experienced tremendous growth over the last two decades as a result of the necessary retooling of the American workforce as we transition away from manufacturing-based economy to a services-based economy. How will this growth benefit you? Easy! Where there are students, we need faculty. When we say higher ed, though, we are referring to all post-secondary institutions. While we know many of you have your eye on one prize: the tenure-track faculty line, but we encourage you, for the sake of your job-seeking sanity, to remember that there are many more jobs out there that are equally stable and fulfilling. Ask yourself: why do I want a tenure-track job anyway? What does it mean? Many struggle with that question in today's academy because the system of tenure is under constant scrutiny and there is an ever- diminishing number of tenure-track positions posted. The trend is pretty clear. It might be more productive to focus on finding jobs rather than tenure. Why make tenure the goal before you've even landed a position?

Enrollment in Higher Education by Degree Area

Years	Undergraduate*	Graduate	Professional**
2011:	16,871,440	2,841,260	397,918
2019:	18,995,370	3,412,781	421,980

*two-year institutions 7,212,424; 8,185,551
**includes M.D.'s, J.D.'s.

(Source Chronicle of Higher Education)

In 2011, 74,700 doctorates were awarded. I can hear some of you now: *74,700 PhDs! Most of them are probably in my field!* Relax! Doctorates are awarded in a variety of areas. In descending order, the largest numbers of doctorates are awarded in: 1) life sciences; 2) physical sciences; 3) engineering; 4) social sciences; 5) education; 6) humanities; 7) other fields. Only half of the doc students enrolled in PhD programs are likely to complete the program and get the degree. Several will end only with Master's degrees or other specialist degrees or licenses. You're a select group. Be proud, own it, work it.

How about some more numbers? If those numbers aren't impressive enough, take a look at these enrollment figures from *The Chronicle of Higher Education*:

- **China:** 25,346,000
- **U.S.:** 17,759,000
- **India:** 13,930,000

Do you know how to say *wow* in Chinese? And that's only three countries. Looks like a lot of students to me. Who's going to teach them all? You! (Well not all, but at least a few.) And one last set of numbers that's equally important: degrees awarded in US graduate programs. Why is this important? Well, who else can teach MAs, PhDs, MDs, and JDs but others with the same initials. You're a precious commodity, and don't you forget it. The number of graduate students enrolled in master's and doctoral programs continues to climb. Information is power, some say. The more you know about the numbers, the better you'll be at playing the odds.

Degrees Awarded

Years	2011	2015	2019
Master's	**696,000**	**771,000**	**839,000**
Doctorate	**74,700**	**86,300**	**979,000**
Professional	**102,300**	**110,600**	**121,900**

(Source Chronicle of Higher Education)

Even if you're not a math person, you're likely to see the trend. If not we'll spell it out: Higher Ed is growing. You are getting a degree in demand. Most PhD's feel very uncomfortable with the idea of marketing or selling themselves to potential employers, to search committees. It is essential for new graduates as well as experienced professionals to develop a thorough, well-defined plan to promote their qualifications, experiences, skills, talents and personalities. You undoubtedly feel confident that the knowledge and competencies acquired in graduate school have prepared you for a professional position. However sophisticated as you may be about the intricacies of your chosen field, you may feel inadequately prepared and uneasy about the prospect of finding suitable employment opportunities and getting hired in a competitive market.

> *"Academics can sell their topic and their research interests to anyone. Trying to sell themselves to a search committee is a totally different beast. New doc students need to think about this."*
> ~Associate Professor, Economics

It's not that you are afraid of competition. You have competed for grades and recognition throughout your graduate school experience, but the competition you now face for available positions in your fields will undoubtedly be even more intense and, for most individuals, will have far greater consequences. Like your graduate program, the process by which people are selected for academic and professional positions can be seen as a linear progression.

Unlike your graduate studies, however, which were designed in such a way that successful completion of each stage of the outlined program would lead you much closer to your goal, the course of your job search is usually determined and executed on your own, relying on your own judgment and your own particular skills, adapted to your unique preferences and requirements. It can be a lonely process, but it doesn't have to be. Approach your job search in the same deliberate way you move through your graduate program. A marketing plan can help.

Establishing your Marketing Plan

Students reading this book from degree programs in business or marketing may be well aware of the tenets of a marketing plan. The rest of us, who spent our graduate years debating Kafka's, *Metamorphosis,* have no idea about the difference between external and internal marketing analyses, and contribution margin analysis: forget it! We're going to make it simple and present the basis for a functional marketing plan that's straightforward, deliberate, and maximizes and focuses your output so that you don't get caught in the wrong distribution channel (ha!). Just trust us. The fundamentals of your academic job search marketing plan include:

1. **Knowing you: Are you a researcher, teacher, or both**
   (Hey, this is you! That special features thing is important too...even though you're in a select group, you have to still stand out.)
2. **Knowing your marketing budget**
   (What will this job search cost you? Materials, time, self-esteem, marriage?)
3. **Knowing the marketing context: the ins and outs of your academic job search and ways to nuance yourself**
   (Online, in person, through the grapevine, professional networks, and knowing which tactics to employ in each of those settings.)
4. **Knowing your pricing strategy: your worth, your market**
   (What's your worth? Have your advisor do an appraisal.)

Who are you? Teacher-Scholar or Scholar-Teacher

No marketing plan is complete without thorough knowledge of you, the product you're selling. The description of you should be found in all of your materials: teaching philosophy, research plan, writing samples, cover letters, and, of course, your curriculum vitae (CV). Your identity as an academic will encompass three primary areas: teaching, research, and service. You'll want to craft a mission statement so that it addresses those three areas. Sure, each institution weights these three key components of academia differently, but all institutions will require something of each to a degree. The description of you that you share with others should certainly be relevant to the needs of the academy, your field, and your discipline.

> *"Job seekers need to decide well before they get to the job-seeking stage, whether they are teacher-scholars or scholar-teachers."*
> ~Chair, Higher Education and Student Affairs

This part of your plan, of course, takes into account those aspects of your professional identity that are unique, specialized and highly marketable. Stop right now if you believe you have no marketable skills. Think about the others in your department. Do a comparison. How are you better than them? Where do you fall short? It's time for academic show and tell. It's time to count your publications because search committees will be, and it's time to haul out your research and teaching philosophies. How do you distinguish yourself? How do you describe yourself?

Marketing Budget

Academic job searches are an investment in time and money. Your advisor has probably told you that job searches are time-intensive enterprises but they may not have indicated that you should skimp a bit this year on the summer vacation get-away to Las Vegas with the other grad students. The costs of a job search can catch many off guard. While not insurmountable, the simple materials necessary for a successful search can add loads of stress to already stressed-out job seekers.

The money you spend during a job search is nothing compared to the expenses you've incurred pursuing your degree. There really is no way to avoid some cash outlay here, so plan ahead and put a bit away for your job search. There are several hidden expenses: for example, a hiring department may require that you open an account with a credentialing agency to submit materials. Suddenly that freebee CV may cost you a few bucks to upload. Another common unanticipated cost is the initial outlay of travel expenses. You've been invited to three campus visits. Each will reimburse you for flights, hotels, and other expenses: *after your visit!* Most of us don't have enough money to visit our folks at Thanksgiving, let alone travel to three different campuses in the US. Oh, and don't forget about taking the dog to the kennel, and the meds you have to put her on for anxiety. Suddenly, you're bankrupt and dealing with a neurotic dog before you've even left the state. Unintended side effects of an academic job search: Canine Neurosis. Here are some costs of the academic job search, some of which are reimbursed, but which may require your initial outlay.

- *Webhosting for ePortfolio*
- *Postage/Printing*
- *Interview/Conference wardrobe*
- *Travel to professional meetings*
- *Transcripts*
- *Campus interview airfare/travel*
- *Campus visit hotel*
- *Computer equipment*
- *Professional memberships*
- *Credentialing agency*

Don't be surprised by unexpected expenses as a part of your search.

The cost of a job search will be influenced by the availability of positions in your field and the scope of your search. The cash outlay required can be minimal or it can run to several thousand dollars. Be prepared for this expense when you launch your professional marketing campaign. Pay off your credit card a year before you begin your search. Candidates get so caught up in the act of job seeking that sometimes the emotional costs are neglected or ignored much to the detriment of the individuals who are important to them. As you launch your marketing campaign, think about whether you are ready for the following *"real"* costs of an academic job search (cue sappy music):

Am I ready ...

- **To have open communication**
  with my faculty, family, and others?
- **To ask for the help I'll need**
  from faculty letter writers, colleagues, family and friends?
- **To invest the necessary time**
  on the road, at conferences, at interviews?
- **To focus**
  and get what I came for? (PhD, Job)
- **To be rejected**
  if I don't manage to get called or invited to campus? (A night of binge drinking can get costly.)
- **To move**
  and start my (or our) life somewhere else. It's never too early to start making plans for your exit strategy.

Understanding Marketing Context

Your marketing plan should consider the different venues in which you'll need to promote and nuance yourself: online social networks (LinkedIn, Facebook), ePortfolios, face-to-face networking opportunities at professional conferences and meetings, and word of mouth. Each one requires slightly different tactics and strategies to make it work. Bottom line: your marketing strategy should be comprehensive and cover all possible venues. Yep, even if you hate Facebook or LinkedIn it may be time to cave in so you don't seem like a cave man! Take a look at the following marketing tools to help you establish a presence.

• *LinkedIn, Facebook, Twitter*	• *Curriculum vitae*
• *Professional associations*	• *Cover letter*
• *Department bio page and websites*	• *Word of mouth*
• *Blogs, online forums, wikis*	• *ePortfolio*
• *Graduate student groups*	• *Journals*

Understand the different ways in which each tool functions. Facebook might not be the place to post a chapter of your dissertation, but you could certainly use Facebook to post a link to your ePortfolio, online dissertation data, or your abstract. Twitter is also excellent for quick networking within many academic communities. Find out if your academic community is active on Twitter and start making tweets (and friends). Your CV, either the full unabridged version, or your short and sweet one-pager, makes an excellent marketing tool when done right (*See CV Handbook: A curriculum vitae owner's manual, PhD Books, 2011*).

But not all of your contact with employers occurs over social networks or via your CV. You'll also need to pay close attention to your behavior as you meet potential employers face-to-face at conferences, through your participation in professional meetings, and, in the end, while you're courting each other during the academic job search. Knowing the ins and outs of the screening process, campus visits, and the offer/negotiations process is key to your success. Each of these kinds of conversations (screening interviews, campus visits, and offers) has their own distinct purpose and protocol that you're expected to follow.

Pricing: Your Academic Capital

Your entire approach to the job search should be built around a realistic analysis of your potential on the academic market. Two candidates from the same program may have vastly different credentials when they enter the market: one has published several research articles, the other has taught every class in the department but no published articles. Is one better than the other? Well, some institutions will say so. Some departments will value the publishing, while others will value extensive teaching.

Apply for the right kinds of jobs: the ones that match your credential so you have something to actually negotiate. If you don't look like the candidate they want on paper (publications, grant funding, teaching, research projects) you probably won't get the invitation to campus in the first place. If getting the invitation to campus isn't the goal for each and every job to which you apply, there is absolutely no reason to apply.

It's bad job-search karma to apply for positions that don't fit with your qualifications and to go through the interview process with this knowledge. Academics keep good company with one another.

We shudder when we hear candidates mention that they probably wouldn't go someplace, or they know it's a long shot, or that they know it's outside of their discipline but they applied anyway. What are you smoking? Who has time for this? It's bad job-search karma, and a bad investment of your time and the search committee's energy.

Institutional Fit

Applying for jobs may be one of the most tedious, emotionally exhausting, and annoying tasks known to the human species. It's pitiful. By the end of the process, many doc students are malnourished, have bags under their eyes, are practically on the verge of divorce, and from the moment they wake up until they hit the bed again (usually 18-20 hours later) they're wondering why someone didn't tell them grad school would be this miserable. So, since we just hate seeing doc students miserable, we hope to convince you that it's really only as bad as you (and you're advisor) make it: make sure you pick a good one.

Once you have determined that you are ready to begin a job search and have begun to assemble a dossier that will support your applications, you need to think about job possibilities. Most doctoral programs fall short of exposing their PhDs to different kinds of work environments: colleges or universities with different missions, or even work outside the academy. If you're like most doc students, your knowledge of what it's like on different campuses probably stems from your direct experience at that far-out undergraduate liberal arts college. If you are seeking an academic position, employment possibilities can be explored at a wide range of institutions from small independent or faith-based colleges to the prestigious and highly selective private universities, and from state-supported schools in rural areas to the huge metropolitan campuses.

> *"You need to understand your values and your own academic mission before you apply for jobs. Don't waste your time or the time of others for positions that are not a good 'institutional match'."*
>
> ~Program Chair, History Department

Your own educational experiences will undoubtedly influence your perceptions and attitudes about various kinds of postsecondary institutions. Considering all viable opportunities will allow you to apply for positions at academic institutions offering various levels of degrees. If you're completing a PhD program, an MFA, or other terminal degree, you are likely well aware of the differences in both program quality to the overall work environment and expectations. The academy is in a major state of transition and reorganization and faculty roles and responsibilities as well as measures of accountability are changing. Faculty at large research institutions may be expected to publish as many as two to three articles in peer-reviewed journals each year with a light course load, while their peers at community colleges may have no publishing expectations but instead teach four to five courses each semester.

Institutions Granting Graduate Degrees

Institutions granting graduate degrees include large research institutions that garner millions in grants each year, to institutions with less of a research focus, but who still offer graduate programming. The variation among these institutions is quite noticeable with faculty at large research institutions expected to carry out a rigorous and productive research agenda that often includes procuring external funding. Faculty at the regional institutions, while still expected to engage in a productive research agenda, might have less in the way of expectations for publishing or securing external funding.

> ***A day in the life: Large State Research University***
> *Doctor So Ahn So works at a large state research university. Her department offers an undergraduate degree in her field, an undergraduate interdisciplinary certificate, a master's level degree program, and a PhD program. She is responsible for coordinating the undergraduate program and her department's involvement in the interdisciplinary certificate program. In addition to teaching two courses a semester (one undergraduate and one graduate course), she advises all undergraduate majors in her area. Because of her specialty and reputation for being an outstanding dissertation advisor, she sits on nearly half of the dissertations in her area. The undergraduate population for both major/minor and interdisciplinary certificate is nearly 400 students, many of whom receive some sort of advising from her. She has a robust research program which includes supervising four graduate research assistants, coordinating a national meeting in her discipline with partner institutions on the grant (25) and publishing and presenting primarily at two national/international conferences, but because her research findings of late have been particularly noteworthy she's been on the road at about one major conference a month. She is involved in serious service commitments at the departmental and collegiate level.*

> ***A day in the life: Regional Teaching University***
> *Doctor Waldo works in a large department that offers two undergraduate majors (one interdisciplinary) and a master's degree. Doctor Waldo contributes regularly to a nationally known blog and website in the field. She is a co-investigator on a state grant that involves other state agencies. She teaches three undergraduate courses a semester, advises a small number of students with one major in her department. She is expected to participate on at least one department, one college-level, and one university-level committee. She is also expected, though never was this written in her contract, to supervise an overseas field experience every other summer. While she doesn't have the same research and publications expectations as Doctor So Ahn So at Large State, she's noticed that the folks in her department who do seem to do the most publishing (both in peer-reviewed and professional newsletters), seem to be promoted faster.*

Colleges and universities that offer graduate programs typically only hire faculty members with terminal degrees in the given field. At institutions with a heavy emphasis on research, you will be expected to have a productive and lively research program. This most often includes obtaining substantial external funding, supporting graduate assistantships with such funding, publishing in peer-reviewed and the top-tier journals in the field. Faculty members may teach graduate as well as undergraduate classes, conduct advanced seminars, and participate in supervision of theses and dissertations. While very important, teaching will often play second fiddle to your research identity. Service to the department and college is important, but often the real service the administration would like to see is in your field to/for the profession (journal editor, association president, reviewer for national conference or accreditation). Do you see yourself as Dr. So Ahn So or Dr. Waldo?

Not all institutions with graduate programs are equal in terms of how they emphasize the work of the faculty (research, teaching, and service) nor are they equal in terms of student body and demographics. Some faculty will work solely with graduate populations and some faculty in the same department may even work only with undergraduates. It's important for you to understand where you'd like your emphasis to be: research or teaching, and then secondarily, your ideal student population: graduate, undergraduate, professionals, and international students. You'll need to think about this not only during the application process, but also during the interview when you are asked questions about what you'll bring to the particular institution.

Institutions Granting Baccalaureates as the Highest Degree

Four-year colleges and universities that don't offer graduate programming are as different as the students who attend them: campuses with a religious affiliation, men's or women's colleges, art and fashion institutes, specialized degrees and programs, alternative course formats (online, one course at a time campuses, courses at sea, international programs). Faculty members may be responsible for upper or lower-division courses, honors seminars/workshops, or supervision of independent study. Research may be encouraged, but greater emphasis is usually placed upon classroom instruction.

Depending on the circumstances of the particular institution, faculty may find themselves heavily invested and involved in student success initiatives, student advising, supervision of student groups, a high level of community exposure and involvement. There tends to be a pervasive belief that faculty in these institutions are not required to publish, though we find that most do have some sort of both spoken and unspoken expectation that they are actively involved in their discipline and participate in opportunities that are especially relevant and beneficial for the environment in which they teach. This might be serving on special interest groups, coordinating a consortium of like colleges, departments, or units. The key mantra on these campuses is simple: student success and engagement on campus and a successful student transition to the workplace or graduate studies. A faculty member adept at student programming and success initiatives in addition to an interdisciplinary collaborator finds this environment quite rewarding.

Institutions Granting Associates as the Highest Degree

The growth of community college enrollments in the last decade has far outpaced that of other institution types. What does this mean for you? Well, it means that there are lots of jobs to be had at community colleges. It's not uncommon for community college faculty to teach anywhere from 4-5 courses a semester. In addition to the large teaching load, community college faculty members are involved in committee and curriculum work. They often do their own advising, and most must maintain a relatively flexible work schedule offering courses when it's convenient for students (online, at night, weekends).

Faculty members are responsible for instruction of students in a two-year associate degree programs. Programs may be terminal or designed as lower-division courses for students who transfer to institutions awarding baccalaureate degrees. Most often, classroom teaching is emphasized and a master's degree is usually a minimum requirement for employment, though more and more community colleges are seeking PhDs to fill their ranks.

There are several myths that surround teaching in community colleges. Let's take just a moment to debunk a few for this simple reason: it's our belief that unless you will be completely heartbroken if you don't land a tenure-track research job, teaching in community colleges can lead to a wonderful life, that yes, unbeknownst to most, includes tenure. Another pervasive belief is that community colleges don't pay much more than high school teaching jobs. Have you seen what teachers make lately? Salaries at community colleges are, for the most part, highly competitive with similar benefit, retirement, and (the best part) schedule as most colleges and universities. Most community colleges offer a full schedule of summer classes. This means more opportunity for you to earn money doing what you love.

Non-"PROF" Professional Opportunities

While most of you have your heart and soul in locating a teaching or research position, preferably on the tenure track, we'd be selling you short if we failed to point out the myriad professional opportunities that exist at most institutions. From grants-based research opportunities to student success and development programming, there are multiple ways to engage your specialized skillset in knowing this place like the back of your hand. You've been learning the ins and outs of the academy and your discipline for the last several years. If you struggle to find a teaching or research position or, in fact, if you desire to not find a teaching or research position, consider working in one of these related fields.

- *Student Services*
- *Research Laboratory*
- *International Programs*
- *Resident Life*
- *Grants & Scholarships Office*
- *Student Health*
- *Computer/Software Helpdesk*
- *Recreation Services*
- *Academic Support Services*
- *Athletics Support Services*
- *Academic Tutoring*
- *Financial Aid*
- *Advising & Career Services*
- *Information Technology Services*

Private and community-based organizations may offer similar opportunities. Corporations regularly seek to hire the best and brightest in the field to conduct research and administrative activities. While many new PhDs scoff at the idea of working anywhere but academe, many find life outside the Ivory Tower to be refreshing, non-bureaucratic, and highly lucrative. In the last several years, because of fiscal pressures, an increasing number of academics sought positions outside of academe. The benefits of experiences outside of the academy have been well-documented, and we imagine that many of these individuals will be successful in their bid to return to the academy someday.

"Our role as academic advisors is to help our students find the right fit. The right fit for some doctorates is not in academe but in policy making, think tanks, in the corporate world. It's important to recognize the skill-set of the advisee and guide them correctly."

~American Studies Professor, Women Studies

Employment opportunities for PhDs exist in local, state, and federal government agencies. Typical jobs for persons with advanced degrees include positions as administrators, managers, researchers, analysts, content specialists, program developers, consultants, and trainers. Positions may become available at any time during the year and many federal agencies hire from occupational registers compiled by the Office of Personnel Management. However, agencies such as the Library of Congress, the Federal Bureau of Investigation, the Central Intelligence Agency, and the National Security Agency should be contacted directly for application information.

Decoding Job Descriptions

After you have determined the scope of your job search, including the types of positions and geographic locations you will consider, you can begin to look for announcements in academic and professional journals, newsletters, and professional publications. All academics should be familiar with *The Chronicle of Higher Education*, but are you aware of the other resources that address issues in higher ed? Bookmark the following resources:

	Selected Resources: Jobs & College Contact Information
	The Chronicle of Higher Education Washington, DC: The Chronicle of Higher Education http://www.chronicle.com
	College Community Times Washington, DC: American Association of Community Colleges http://www.communitycollegetimes.com
	Community College Week Fairfax, VA: Autumn Publishing Enterprises, Inc. http://www.ccweek.com
	The College Handbook New York, NY: The College Board http://store.collegeboard.com
	Directory of Canadian Universities = Répertoire des universités canadiennes Ottawa, Ontario: Association of Universities/Colleges of Canada http://www.aucc.ca/can_uni/index_e.html
	HigherEdJobs Oak Park, IL http:www.higheredjobs.com
	Higher Education Directory Falls Church, VA: Higher Education Publications, Inc. http://www.hepinc.com
	INSIDE Higher ED Washington, DC http://www.insidehighered.com
	International Handbook of Universities (was World List of Universities) London, England: Pelgrave MacMillan http://www.palgrave.com/home
	The World of Learning London, England: Europa Publishing, Ltd http://www.worldoflearning.com

Most universities list openings on their college or university website. If you have a preferred geographic location, bookmark all the post-secondary institutions in the area and check back on a regular basis to see if new positions have been added. As you filter your search results, you have ultimately two tasks: a) to get to know the institution, especially if it's one you're not terribly familiar with (size, student profile, faculty profile, endowment) and; b) take a close look at the job advertisement, paying particular attention to both stated and some inferred conclusions or assumptions you could make about the given job. Take a look at the job description below and the discussion that follows.

Sample faculty job announcement

Big State Research University

Assistant/Associate Professor of Sociology and Criminal Justice

Big State Research University College of Business, Arts and Sciences seeks nominations and applications for a full-time faculty position with an appointment effective August 201x. Rank: Assistant/Associate professor; Salary: commensurate with level of experience and qualifications. Nine month appointment.

Responsibilities include teaching courses in sociology and criminal justice. The person who is hired will need to use and teach quantitative and qualitative methods specific to the social and behavioral sciences, and will work collaboratively within the division on faculty and student research. Candidate will be expected to provide leadership in the discipline as the College grows its program. In addition, participation on appointed committee assignments, academic advising, and recruitment activities within the Division will be expected.

Required Qualifications

- Doctorate (or ABD) in the field
- Quantitative/qualitative background for research/data analysis class
- Demonstrated passion for and effectiveness in teaching with a strong commitment to student interaction in a liberal arts context

Preferred Qualifications

- Some teaching experience at the college level
- Established research agenda particularly in mixed methods research
- Earned Doctorate

Applications

Visit the website to complete the online application. Materials to be uploaded include: a CV; letter expressing interest in the job; research agenda; statement of teaching experience, interests and philosophy; all transcripts; and the contact information for three references. Initial review of applications will begin on January 5, 201x and will continue until the position in filled. The department embraces a commitment to faculty diversity.

Title/Level of Position

Familiar ranks include: instructor, assistant professor, associate professor and professor. Other common academic titles include lecturer, researcher, fellow, visiting professor, clinical professor (assistant to full), artist or writer-in-residence. Rank and titles are established by guidelines covering qualifications, previous experiences, and descriptions of performance requirements. As a general rule, first-time job-seekers will be considered for entry-level positions carrying the title of assistant professors. Faculty positions above the entry level usually carry the title of associate professor or professor. To receive serious consideration of these senior positions, the applicant must hold an equivalent rank or have an outstanding record of achievement in a position of lower rank. Similarly, titles of nonacademic employment in social services agencies, clinics, hospitals, libraries, and state or federal government departments and offices may vary greatly and are not necessarily indicative of the nature of the duties and responsibilities assigned. Do not rule out any job possibility simply on the basis of the title.

In the Big State Research University (BSRU) advertisement, the position posted is an assistant/associate professor: that means it's tenure-track. What's not clear is whether the appointment is split between two departments. Are Sociology and Criminology one department? You could be dealing with double the meetings if they are not. Even though the job announcement indicates that ABD may apply, because BSRU is ready to hire open rank (meaning either assistant or associate) it's a bit of a long shot, but in today's academy, you know when the right person comes along.

Term of Appointment

The announcement will state the term or the duration of the position. In cases where the position is temporary, the announcement should include such phrases as "one-year replacement position," "sabbatical replacement," "three-year, fixed-term appointment," or even "contingent upon continued funding." For most academics, the most desirable or sought-after positions are those that offer the possibility of a permanent appointment or continuing contract, typically designated as "tenure-track" positions. To obtain tenure, an academic must meet the criteria established by the institution within a specified number of years. Traditionally, tenure has been awarded to those who demonstrate excellence in teaching, research, and academic or community service. Today, tenure considerations may also include the individual's national or even international reputation as a scholar or leader in the field.

At BSRU, the announcement clearly spells out full-time, tenure-track. The ad also indicates the job is a nine-month appointment. This means you'll have summers to do your research and prepare for teaching.

Responsibilities and Duties

Most announcements are quite specific about the duties and responsibilities of the position. Use the information presented to your best advantage. You'll find inspiration for your cover letter in this section. This is what they want you to do. It may not be worth your time or effort to apply for jobs for which you are obviously not qualified, but if you are qualified for the major portion of the described responsibilities and you hold the required degree you should consider submitting your application.

At BSRU, an entire paragraph is devoted to your responsibilities, including: methodologies you'll be expected to teach, kinds of collaboration, student research, leadership, academic advising, committee appointments, and recruitment activities. Your questions for the sake of understanding whether you'll fit are: How many students will I be advising? What does student research mean (graduate/undergraduate, paid/unpaid)? What does recruitment mean? Where do BSRU's students originate?

Required or Preferred Qualifications

Most announcements state that a terminal degree or its equivalent is required or preferred. You might even see the phrase, "ABD considered." This means folks who are nearly complete with their programs, thus *all but dissertation* may apply for the job. Your advisor may strongly discourage you from leaving before finished with your program as some joke that ABD really stands for "all but dead," meaning many who leave their programs before completing never actually finish the PhD. It's a risky proposition, but one that may be necessary given your circumstances.

In most fields, the master's degree is not considered a terminal degree. The MFA in the visual and performing arts and the doctorate in any field are considered terminal degrees. Requirements or preferences for experience may also be stated. If an announcement indicates that experience is necessary, you will probably not be considered unless you can demonstrate at least the equivalent of the stated requirement. Concentrate your energies on applying for positions for which you meet or exceed the stated minimum requirements.

At BSRU, the required qualifications are clearly spelled out. It's the preferred qualifications that give us some hints into what these folks are looking for: someone done with the PhD (they need this person to be focused and done); maybe who's been teaching for a few years (experience teaching at College level) as a visiting faculty member, etc.; and someone who really specializes in mixed methods research. Most search committees, like the one at BSRU, have a niche that the candidate needs to fill.

Starting Date

Job announcements for academic settings, whether for faculty or staff positions, will indicate a starting date. The starting dates for teaching positions are rarely negotiable. Research or professional staff positions can allow some latitude or flexibility and starting dates are often indicated as, for example, "January 1 or as soon as possible thereafter." To hire the most qualified applicant, most employers will adjust the starting date if an adjunct or temporary professor can be located and appointed.

Application Deadline

Pay careful attention to stated deadlines for submitting application materials. Some announcements clearly indicate that all materials (letter, CV, dossier, portfolio) must be received by a certain date; others may simply indicate a closing date with no specific instructions. Follow directions carefully and make every effort to comply with the employer's request. Missing a deadline may not only put you at a disadvantage, it may completely eliminate your application from consideration. No, the folks at BSRU weren't just suggesting January 5 as a deadline. They mean it.

Salary

Salary information is rarely stated in figures on a job announcement. If it is, most commonly, a range or starting salary is provided, or the salary is described as negotiable or commensurate with qualifications and experience. At this point don't worry about salary, just apply for the job.

At BSRU, no specific figure is quoted, but because it's a large state research institution, there are likely figures and benchmarks that may be available publically. The notion that salary is commensurate with experience means that those hired as associates will, of course, be compensated more for their previous experience than will those who enter at the assistant level. Try not to make salary the focus at this stage of the game. Get the job first.

Notes

Notes

Tools of the Trade

PhD Planner

PART 2: TOOLS OF THE TRADE

Part 2 of *The PhD Handbook for the Academic Job Search* focuses on preparing the marketing tools you'll need to get the attention of search committees. In this section you'll learn about common tools for job search success, including: the curriculum vitae, also known as the CV, the cover letter, teaching philosophies, research statements and agendas, the interview portfolio and ways that you can utilize social media to get the word out about you: the next star of academe!

8	**Letters of Recommendation** Who can speak to my potential as a scholar?
9	**Transcripts** Evidence of degree attainment
10	**Marketing Tools** My scholarly proof
11	**Letter and Application Log** Staying on top of your applications
12	**Teaching Philosophy Inventory** Knowing your stuff as a teacher
13	**Teaching Philosophy Profile** My beliefs on teaching and learning in the academy
14	**Teaching Agenda** In a perfect world, I'd teach...
15	**Research Inventory** Because knowing your research matters
16	**Research Profile** My beliefs on research in my field
17	**Portfolio Checklist** Showcasing my goods

The Curriculum Vitae (CV)

The academic job search usually begins in earnest something like this. You stumble out of bed after having had a long night of analyzing your dissertation data. You walk to the kitchen, which is still a complete mess with Chinese take-out and bits and pieces of your dissertation data practically everywhere. You turn on the coffee pot and begin clearing a small space for yourself at the kitchen table by removing the "table cloth" of research articles, dissertation data, and failed attempts at chapter 2. You grab your Mac to see what the latest buzz on Facebook is. Of course, since no one has posted since you last looked five hours ago (because none of your friends are up yet, nor do many of them enjoy your academic schedule) you check your email and you see it: the dream job. The job you've been hoping for since you started this long journey several years ago. You feel your heart rate increase, beads of sweat begin to form on your crown, your hands start to feel shaky. Wait. It's not because of the job, it's that ridiculously strong blend from Starbucks. You read the job description over and over, and it ends like this:

> **Application Process**
> Candidates should submit to the search committee:
> 1. **Curriculum vitae**
> 2. **Letter of interest**
> 3. **Three confidential letters of recommendation**
> 4. **Dissertation abstract & writing sample**
> 5. **Teaching philosophy and research statement**
> 6. **Transcripts of all graduate and undergraduate degrees**

Today's academic marketing tools include these basic items: (1) the CV and/or professional résumé; (2) letters of recommendation; (3) portfolio materials, including at a minimum, your philosophy statement, research agenda, writing samples, teaching evaluations, and syllabi. Without exception, anyone seeking a position in higher education or in various service professions, must develop and use effectively these job-seeking tools.

When was the last time you updated your CV? I mean, you knew this was coming and that you should have been updating it, but you realize the last time you updated that thing was for the graduate student travel award you applied for last year. You have everything covered, but realize you need to spend the rest of the morning updating your CV. Time to put on the coffee and get to work.

A *curriculum vitae* or CV, as it is commonly abbreviated, is an academic's perpetual, though forever unfinished, companion. Throughout the course of a career, a CV is frequently required: as a part of the screening process for virtually all teaching and research appointments; in support of candidacy for promotion or tenure; to accompany funding or grant applications, manuscript submissions; nominations for leadership positions, academic or professional honors. This ubiquitous document is an integral part of any request for employment, recognition, or reward. So what is a CV?

▶ **CV:**

Curriculum vitae or CV is most commonly defined as a summary of one's personal history and professional qualifications, as that submitted by a job applicant (Webster's New Twentieth Century Dictionary). A CV is an academic version of a résumé used within the academic and research communities. Featured in CVs are degrees earned, certificates, research skills and lab experience, teaching experience, publications, presentations, abstracts, technical reports, international projects, languages, exhibitions, and related activities. Typically, length is dictated by the content, so one CV may be two pages, another may be 20 pages or more.

And for those of you who need a résumé for a professional job:

▶ **RÉSUMÉ:**

A résumé is a document that summarizes education, experience qualifications, skills, special talents and other items related to the writer's objective. Legitimate entries could include particular coursework, non-academic pursuits, and civic or community activities. Typically, a résumé is one to two pages in length, although this can vary with degrees, life-experiences and industry type.

Ideally, you've at least started your CV. You had to use one to get into graduate school, so chances are you're not starting completely from scratch. Candidates come to us all the time with concern about the length of their CV: *it just doesn't seem long enough.* While it is true that the CV of an experienced professor typically consists of numerous pages of accomplishments that seem unreachable by you, your CV's length will be determined by the content. Although the length of a CV can become an issue for novices and veterans, the difference between the CV of a relative beginner and a senior professor is not just in the number of pages it encompasses. Search committees understand that the NSF probably isn't doling out mega-grants to graduate students, nor will most of you have a long list of publications in the top-rated journal in your field. They do, however, expect some evidence that you can *eventually* get grants and get published. Your CV is all about demonstrating your trajectory for success in your field. Ambitious graduate students have worked to get some publications out, even if just in that obscure graduate student newsletter. Likewise, they've worked to get mini-grants, travel awards, and other kinds of funding that requires both initiative and submission of a proposal or paperwork. You are expected to be an independent scholar and your CV must demonstrate an ability to be independently productive.

Length Matters: The length must be determined by the content and the content must be governed by the purpose for which the CV is prepared.

At this point in the game, it's too late to join every professional organization or try adding teaching and research experiences that you missed out on two years ago. Likewise, by now you should be well aware of the lengthy publication submission process. Chances are you have more than you think you do. It never fails during a professional consultation that a doc students says, "Oh yeah," or, "I forgot about that!" or, "I didn't know I could include that," or, my personal favorite, "Search committees want to know that?" My answer, YES! Just bare it all on your CV (but remember - no pictures please.)

So what goes into your CV? How do you best relate your varied experiences to specific positions? Many students visit us with specific job descriptions in hand. Their thought is that they need to craft a unique CV for each position. Our advice to them: unless you want to be on anti-psychotics by the end of the semester, it's probably not worth your time or effort to reinvent the wheel for each job. A little tweaking here or there (not of the psychedelic variety) is fine based on the knowledge you possess about decoding the job description. Making sure you touch on all critical points and address each of the hiring department's needs. Most often the tweaking and fine tuning you'll engage in should amount to nothing more than a different verb here or there and potentially reordering a research/teaching interests or experiences to highlight those attributes that are most salient. Take a look at the following sections of your CV.

Contact Information and Education

Your contact information shouldn't upstage your education section. Too many graduates use EGO sized font for their name and contact information. Most of you will be applying via an online application portal anyway. Rarely will a search committee use the contact information provided on your CV to contact you, so let's not make this section rocket science. Keep it simple: name, address, cell number, email. Done. If you leave a cell number remember to check your greeting. It should be professional and short. When you're job seeking, being away from your email is non-optional. Vacation messages can steer your search committee to the next candidate. Your education section should begin with your highest degree earned or in progress (namely the PhD, MFA, MD, DDS, etc.). Basically, the degree that will get you the job is the one that's most important here. If the graduate degree is recent or still in progress, it is helpful to include the dissertation title or topic. The names of the advisor, principal teachers, or committee members can help to stimulate interest. Comprehensive examination areas can help to define the scope of academic interest and preparation.

Teaching and Research Experiences

Teaching and research responsibilities and experiences can include both assistantships and professional experiences outside the academy. Most of you will have a stronger credential in one or the other. It's good to know where your strengths lie, because search committees depend on your strengths as they carry you through the application and vetting process. Remember, they are looking for the perfect fit for their department. No one gets hired because they are "kind of" a match. In today's financial environment, committees are under greater pressure than ever to make good hires.

The terms teaching and research assistant are relatively vague given the great disparity between what those jobs might look like across campuses and even within departments. Some Teaching Assistants do it all, while some simply grade and take attendance. Likewise, some Research Assistants do data entry, while others are involved in the entire research process from methodology design, to implementation, to data analysis and write up. Annotations should convey the extent of authority and the implication of actual, though pre-professional, experience. Annotations play a key role in defining for the search committee the role you played in your department as an emerging faculty member. Remember, your CV is about your trajectory not about having already done it all. Be specific, yet brief. With hundreds of CVs to read, yours shouldn't be the one that has the search committee's eyes rolling because you're a bit on the verbose side. Your audience after all, is probably a group of pretty smart people. Don't bore them with minor insignificant details, and avoid repetition of verbs.

Publications, Presentations, Leadership & Service

The ticket to just about any academic job is your engagement in the discipline demonstrated most often by your potential as a researcher or public figure in your field. It's not common, nor easy for most graduate students to have a name in the field by the time they graduate, but many have demonstrated strong potential in this direction by a significant list of publications and presentations. A long list of publications and presentations (even if not in peer-reviewed journals or keynotes at your discipline's major annual meeting) demonstrates, in the end, your leadership in the field. Leadership, however, isn't limited to your record of publications and presentations; it also includes departmental committees, leadership of the graduate student body on your campus or in your department, and participating in departmental functions and key campus groups.

In the end, all of this matters, but all too often, folks fail to format this particular section of their CV in a way that helps present a clear message to search committees. Use the formatting convention common to your discipline for listing publications and presentations (MLA, APA, etc.). Don't skimp on this section and don't be overly zealous either. List all publications, even those for that random graduate student newsletter or community bulletin. If you have a substantial list of publications and presentations for a variety of contexts, consider organizing in such a way that is easier for search committees to pay attention to those publications and presentations that they will find significant, while still noticing that you've had a high level of engagement on the community or regional level as well.

Campuses will have different values with respect to service expectations for faculty. Do your homework to understand the kinds of service activities of the faculty in the department to which you're applying. Is service primarily to the department or campus? Does it seem more outwardly directed or associated with the professional association that represents your field? Is your discipline one that has a heavy clinical or community-based programs emphasis? These questions will help you determine the nature of service that your search committee will value. It's your job to align your service experiences with their needs. Too many candidates leave out interesting and often valuable service experiences that seem less academic and therefore non-relevant. It's better to be comprehensive while acknowledging that fine moment when being comprehensive becomes fluff.

A mentor can be helpful in reminding students that academic service is expected as a collegial responsibility. Indications of participation in departmental affairs, search committees, curriculum reviews, or election as a student representative to college or university boards, show evidence of the commitment to contribute to the academic community.

The following short list of categories and entries will help you formulate a strong CV in the area of publications, presentations, leadership and service.

• *Peer-reviewed Articles*	• *National Presentations*
• *Newsletters, Blogs*	• *Publications in Progress*
• *Scientific Papers*	• *Lectures*
• *Recitals, Performances*	• *Poster Session*
• *Articles and Monographs*	• *Panel Participation*
• *Workshops*	• *Invited Speaker*
• *Exhibits, Group Shows*	• *Moderator*
• *Service Learning*	• *Information Technology Services*
• *Volunteer Experiences*	• *Conference Volunteer*
• *Memberships & Affiliations*	• *Community Outreach*

References

The last page of your CV should be a section of professional references. Most higher education institutions will expect that your significant mentors will be listed, including: dissertation chair, committee members, key faculty advisors, and teaching/research assistantship supervisors. It's nice for search committees to know, not only that Dr. So Ahn So is a chaired professor, but how Dr. So Ahn

So relates to you. Take a look at the sample to see how you might provide sufficient details to search committees in your reference listing. You may be asked to provide contact information on an electronic application form. It's most customary to use the same references, although some application forms will specifically direct you to list various individuals by function (dissertation supervisor, teaching/research supervisor). It's imperative that the individuals you list either on your CV or on an electronic application are aware that their names have been provided as references so that they are prepared for the possible screening phone call or email. Notify them in a timely fashion so that they have ample time to prepare your reference and review your CV.

Alec Sample

Advisor:	*Dissertation Chair:*	*Mentor:*
B.E. Example, Ph.D. Director, Research Labs 21 Academic Triangle Any University AnyPlace, State, zip 324.432.5678 (Cell) Be-example@univ.edu	So Ahn So, Ph.D. Smith Distinguished Chair Graduate College Any University AnyPlace, State, zip 304.432.5678 (Cell) So-ahn-so@univ.edu	Ken Duitt, M.D., Ph.D. Distinguished Professor 21 Research Center Any University AnyPlace, State, zip 384.412.5678 (Cell) Ken-duitt@univ.edu

Inappropriate Material for your CV

Not so many years ago, it was standard practice to include information on a CV that is now considered irrelevant and inappropriate. There is no justifiable reason to include date or place of birth, or information about sex, race, religion, spouse or significant other, number of dependents, health, height, weight, or color of eyes and hair. A CV containing this personal data appears either naively old-fashioned or consciously calculated. Regardless of age, experience, or professional status, listing vital statistics is unnecessary, unsophisticated, and usually unwise.

Unless they are somehow connected to scholarly endeavors, categories featuring leisure interests, avocations, political, religious, and civic activities are out of place on a CV. Facebook is a better platform for disclosure of your personal pastimes, but remember most search committee members will also take a gander at the short list of candidates on Facebook and other social media.

> *For many new job seekers, it appears that social media has had an undue influence on what is personal and what is professional. A job search is not about full disclosure but rather, about the professional abilities and knowledge that a candidate can bring to a particular department or college setting."*
>
> ~Chair, Classics Department

It's not entirely to your disadvantage to have a personal web presence (most people would be hard pressed not to) but your level of professionalism or, perhaps better stated, knowledge of appropriate web-etiquette including privacy settings, and if you're completely public, appropriate behavior will be key in any 21st century job search.

CV Basics

Remember that a CV evolves as a career develops; relevance is not constant. Items related to teaching, research or clinical experience as a graduate student need to be reviewed and evaluated in light of postgraduate opportunities, responsibilities, service and scholarly activities.

Use your CV as a professional archive. Remember to add all relevant details regardless of how significant or insignificant they may seem in comparison to your faculty advisor's. You are new to this. We know it.

The CV Handbook by Coghill-Behrends and Anthony covers everything you would ever want to know about the CV. A quick refresher (see below) can give you a clear picture of what is acceptable and what is off-limits on your CV. We know you are busy, so we've made it easy to peruse.

- Represent all dates, degrees, and distinctions with accuracy
- Select a font that is easy to read and reasonable in size (10 or 11pt)
- Select appropriate category headings based on your experiences
- Use action phrases and annotations that are meaningful and powerful
- Use MLA or APA Publication styles
- Name and page number appear on all pages after the first

- Avoid personal information (age, race, weight, religion, marital status)
- Delete social security numbers or other identification numbers
- Put photos of yourself in your family photo album, not your CV
- Non-scholarly activities belong on Facebook
- Date your cover letter, not your CV
- Proof, proof, and have a second set of eyes proof your CV
- High quality prints or scans only please. This is a real job after all.
- Select white paper for CVs used in conference or interview settings
- Electronic CVs should be saved as a high quality PDF

The following CV Checkup Checklist can help you keep your eye on the prize and the focus on your CV development so that you're not wasting valuable time and energy when you should be focusing on getting your dissertation done and getting out of Dodge.

CV CHECKUP CHECKLIST			
	Dates (degrees, presentations)		Spelling
	Grammar		References (names, numbers)
	Updated contact information (name, phone, address)		Checked your cell phone voice mail greeting
	Even margins		Page numbers
	Categories begin and end on same page		Relabeled categories if more than a page is necessary
	Correct contact information		Printed on white paper for conferences
	No dates in header or footers		Don't name your CV "Curriculum Vitae"
	No personal license numbers		Saved as pdfs
	No personal information		One last time, Spellcheck!

Action Words

Keeping the reader awake is *really* important. Your CV must grab the attention of your audience and has the potential, after all, to be one of the most boring documents known to humankind: make it interesting, Make me want to meet you. Powerful action words used effectively in your annotations help describe your experiences in teaching, research, service, program implementation, and other categories. There are no complete sentences in CVs.

How might action words help me demonstrate my potential? Take a look:

> *Conducted applied research in the area of functional communication training and behavioral persistence; assisted in the development of singe case designs and interpretation of data; provided supervision and training of junior graduate student team members; piloted new survey instrument with research participants.*

Action Words:

Accomplished	**Achieved**	**Addressed**
Analyzed	**Arbitrated**	**Arranged**
Assessed	**Authored**	**Briefed**
Built	**Chaired**	**Collaborated**
Commissioned	**Compiled**	**Conducted**
Contributed	**Critiqued**	**Delivered**
Designed	**Developed**	**Directed**
Edited	**Elected**	**Encouraged**
Envisioned	**Established**	**Explored**
Facilitated	**Formulated**	**Fostered**
Generated	**Guided**	**Helped**
Illustrated	**Implemented**	**Improved**
Incorporated	**Integrated**	**Invented**
Judged	**Launched**	**Lectured**
Mobilized	**Moderated**	**Motivated**
Negotiated	**Observed**	**Optimized**
Performed	**Pioneered**	**Presented**
Produced	**Programmed**	**Provided**
Recorded	**Revamped**	**Reviewed**
Selected	**Served**	**Stimulated**
Strengthened	**Supervised**	**Synthesized**
Tailored	**Taught**	**Trained**
Tutored	**Validated**	**Verified**
Volunteered	**Worked**	**Wrote**

CV Categories

You can draw attention to your degrees, scholarly activities, and relevant experiences by selecting meaningful and appropriate category headings. No two CVs are alike; each individual has unique experiences to include on a CV. Hiring committees would have no need to request a CV if every Waldo had the same job-seeking document. Review ***The CV Handbook*** for a complete list.

Academic Background	**Comprehensive Areas**
Academic Overview	**Dissertation**
Academic Training	**Dissertation Title**
Degrees	**Dissertation Topic**
Education	**Master's Project**
Educational Background	**Thesis**
Educational Overview	
Formal Education	**Academic Appointments**
Professional Studies	**Academic Overview**
	Clinical Appointments
Academic Interests	**Current Projects**
Areas of Concentration	**Experience**
Areas of Expertise	**Experience Summary**
Areas of Knowledge	**Faculty Appointments**
Areas of Special Interest	**Faculty Development**
Certification	**Fellowships**
Clinical Experiences	**International Experience**
Clinical Training	**Lectures**
Course Highlights	**Major Teaching & Clinical Appointments**
Educational Highlights	**Non-academic Appointments**
Graduate Fieldwork	**Overview of Experience**
Graduate Practica	**Postdoctoral Appointments**
Licensure	**Research Applications**
	Research Areas
Academic Accomplishments	**Research Interests**
Career Achievements	**Teaching & Research Areas**
Career Highlights	**Teaching Interests**
Clinical Training	**Teaching Strengths**
Consulting Experience	

Institutional Service
Professional Development
Related Experience
Research Overview
Service
University Involvement

Convention Addresses
Editorial Appointments
Editorial Boards
Invited Addresses
Invited Lectures
Lectures and Colloquia
Manuscripts & Research
Multimedia Materials
Reviews
Scholarly Works
Selected Presentations
Selected Publications
Technical Papers
Working Papers
Works in Press
Works in Progress
Works Submitted
Workshop Presentations

Arrangements
Exhibits/Exhibitions
Funded Projects
Grants & Contracts
Grants Held
Group Shows
Papers
Patents
Performances

Presentations
Public Collections
Publications
Recitals
Scores
Sponsored Research
Solo & Group Exhibition
Studio Work

Campus Activities
College Leadership
Committee Leadership
Committees
Conference Leadership

Academic Awards
Activities & Distinctions
Awards
Honors and Awards
Distinctions
Fellowships
Honors
Prizes
Professional Contributions
Recognition
Scholarships

Affiliations
Honorary Societies
Memberships
National Boards
Professional Memberships
Professional Organizations
Scholarly Societies

As we mentioned earlier, your CV is a lifelong companion. As an academic you'll use it for job seeking, promotions, conferences, invited speaking engagements, leadership positions, funding opportunities, reviews and publishing submissions. The CV you submit for that perfect job advertised in this month's Chronicle is not the same one you will take to a conference, submit for a fellowship or scholarship, or include with a grant proposal.

It's a bit of a misnomer that you'll use just one CV during your academic job search. Be sensitive to context. You'll send committees your entire unabridged full-scale CV to fully advertise your experiences and potential in a sea of candidates that will likely include experienced faculty members. However, keep that big one to yourself at conferences: take along a one-page summary CV. You'll keep the conversation focused and those strong interpersonal vibes flowing. If you pass me twenty pages of credentials, you communicate two things, *beginner* and *tree abuser*. Go green, go simple, and take along a shortened conference CV.

- **Unabridged job-seeking version:**
  The content determines the length and your career goal determines the focus of the CV. Are you a teacher-scholar or a scholar-teacher? How you present your academic background and scholarly achievements sends a strong message to the readers. Research areas and teaching interests should appeal to the search committee with the requisite and essential skills you bring to the department. This schema (Degrees, Research/Teaching Interests) allows you to highlight your strengths as a potential colleague.

- **One-page version: fellowships/scholarships/conferences**
  One-page versions are the norm at professional conference interview sites and for many fellowships and scholarship applications. Typically, when interviews are held at conference sites, instructions state that only a one-page CV will be accepted. Similarly, selection boards for fellowships or scholarship committees will ask for a one-page CV (in some cases a two-page CV) that stresses certain qualities they want to see in the candidates. In shaping your one-page CV, you'll need to condense categories to include the basic details of degrees, experience, publications, presentations and leadership.

Sample CV: Doctorate degree in progress

ALEC SAMPLE
16 University Avenue, Any City, State 12345 (101) 555-0101 a-sample@IU.edu

ACADEMIC BACKGROUND

Ph.D. **Comparative Literature**
Indiana University, Bloomington
August 201x – present Projected completion date: May 201x
Projected dissertation topic: *Revolutionary poets in the 1920's*

M.A. **Comparative Literature**
Purdue University, June 201x
Thesis: *Eduardo Pinero: An Analysis of Early Writings*

B.A. **Spanish and Global Studies** *magna cum laude*
Butler University, Indianapolis, June 201x

TEACHING INTERESTS

Narrative Literature
Interpretation of Literature
American Lives
Lyric Poetry

RESEARCH APPOINTMENTS

Research Assistant, Comparative Literature, Indiana University, Fall 201x to present, faculty supervisor, Paul Proff, Ph.D.

TEACHING APPOINTMENTS

English Department, Teaching Assistant, Indiana University, Fall 201x
Courses: American Lives; Lyric Poetry
Designed lectures, small group work, weekly readings as well as exams. Used a variety of multimedia resources to enhance teaching. Maintained and uploaded all teaching materials to iTunes University for easy access for on-campus and on-line students.

Department of Spanish and Portuguese, Teaching Assistant, Purdue University, Summer 201x and Spring 201x
Courses: Spanish I; Spanish II (total of 6 sections)
Created syllabus, designed lectures and exams, and worked closely with other TAs teaching concurrent sections to primarily upper class students. Expanded student experience through immersion activities in surrounding community. Recorded "Stories from the Children," a children's storytelling project for use with first-year Spanish students while second-year students worked to gather stories.

INSTRUCTOR

English Department, Instructor, Distance Education, Indiana University, Fall 201x
Taught two online sections of Narrative Literature.

Community College of SW Indiana, Summer Sessions, 201x; 201x
Taught Spanish I to freshman/sophomore students and Conversational Spanish to adult learners.

TECHNOLOGY INTEGRATION

Online/distance education teaching: Online class management software, blogs, nings, Elluminate Live; started an online hotline to help students with questions regarding course content and technology issues.
Website design and management: Flash, SharePoint, Adobe Suite, HTML5

Sample CV: Doctorate degree in progress, page 2

Sample, page 2

PRESENTATIONS

"Tomorrow's Poets." Paper presented at the 21st International Conference of Poets, Chicago, Illinois. November 201x.
"International Students React to Campus Life." International Education Conference, Indiana University, Bloomington, Indiana. May 201x.

PUBLICATIONS

Sample, A. (201x). *Freshman studies and intercultural expectations.* Manuscript submitted for publication.
Sample, A. (in press). *Learning styles and international students.* International Magazine.
Alot, R., Sample, A., & Fine, B.E. (2010). *International students and poetry: an analysis of affinity.* Journal of Poetry. 36, 122-130.

CAMPUS INVOLVEMENT

Co-chair, Course Review Committee for the course, American Lives. *Recommendations accepted by the General Education Program, 201x.*

Student member, Search Committee for the Vice President of Academic Affairs. *Reviewed application materials; participated in screening and selection process, 201x.*

Member, University Music and Lecture Series Committee. *Responsible for reviewing credentials of proposed lecturers, for securing bids and booking contracts for campus lecturers, 201x – 201x.*

RELATED EXPERIENCE

Tutor, Hispanic Learning Center, summers, 201x – 201x. *Taught English to non-English speaking immigrants in the evening program. Worked with adults and children in small group settings and one-on-one.*

Peace Corps Volunteer, Kingston, Jamaica, 200x – 200x. *Duties included teaching English as a second language in Kingston and mountain towns and villages in community center or churches. Taught all ages.*

PROFESSIONAL AFFILIATIONS

Modern Language Association
Society for Spanish & Portuguese Historical Studies

LANGUAGES

Languages: Spanish, Portuguese, French

RECOGNITION

Kinseth Senior Fellowship for International Dissertation Research
Murray International Scholarship
University Award for Outstanding Conference Paper

PROFESSIONAL MATERIALS

References available upon request

Portfolio available at: www.interfolio.com/portfolio/sample
(View: syllabi, student evaluations, research papers, dissertation abstract, conference presentations, video of classroom teaching, campus activities, and community service)

Sample CV: MFA candidate

[ima sample]
cinema : emerging media : sound : education

(917)881.6331
imasample@gmail.com
www.imasample.com

EDUCATION

Master of Fine Arts Candidate–Film & Video Production — *New York University*
Department of Cinema and Comparative Literature — (expected May 201x)
NYU Arts Fellow

Bachelor of Science–Cinema & Photography — *University of Oregon*
Department of Cinema, Photography, and Media Arts — (awarded May *201x)*
Magna Cum Laude

EXHIBITION / SCREENINGS / LECTURES

201x Ann Arbor Film Festival Ambient Media Curated Show, *Ann Arbor, MI*
PBS: Independent Lens. Public Broadcasting Service. *New York, NY* (Colorist)
92Y Tribeca Gallery Space, *New York, NY*
Deconstruction Tutorial' Lecture. Department of Intermedia, NYU

201x ArtGrease Television Broadcast. Squeaky Wheel, *Buffalo, NY*
INCITE! Journal of Experimental Media & Radical Aesthetics supplemental DVD
Glitch: Investigations. The School of the Art Institute of Chicago, *Chicago, IL*
Semana del Cine Experimental de Madrid. *Madrid, Spain* (As Land Camera Collective)

200x Chicago Underground Film Festival, *Chicago, IL*
Videologia. *Volgograd, Russia*
Eight Films International Artist Collective. www.eightfilms.com
Hollis Frampton's 'A Lecture'. New York State Summer School of the Arts, *Ithaca, NY*

AWARDS / RESIDENCIES

201x NYU Graduate College Thesis Completion Grant
Princess Grace Grant Nominee, *New York, NY*
Pacific Research and Production Grant, *Eugene, OR*

201x Telluride Film Festival Student Symposium, *Telluride, CO*
Residency at the Experimental Television Studio, *Oswego, NY*
Susan Royal Memorial Grant, *Chicago, IL*

200x New York Arts Fellowship, *New York, NY*
Verizon Foundation Work Scholarship, *Eugene, OR*
College Presidential Scholarship, *Eugene, OR*

CURATORIAL

201x Executive Director – Exi Theater, NYU
Director – International Documentary Festival

201x Board of Directors – Experimental Film Festival
Staff Coordinator – Siren Film and Video Festival

Sample CV: MFA candidate, page 2

[ima sample, page 2]

TEACHING EXPERIENCE

201x Teaching Assistantship – Alternate Forms of Distribution, NYU
Responsible for writing an original syllabus, conducting class twice a week, grading papers and other assignments including exhibiting a film festival as a hands-on practicum with 16 students. Of note: festival was in conjunction with a plan of study focusing on the history and application of non-commercial distribution.

201x Teaching Assistantship – Modes Film & Video Production, NYU
Responsible for teaching the basics of image, audio, and post-production as well as cinema production theory. Placed emphasis on exceeding the technical aspects of filmmaking, to the ideology of creating one's first film or video and the possibilities open to the maker therein. Led discussion section and often addressed class of 67.

PROFESSIONAL / SERVICE EXPERIENCE

201x Editing Consultant – *Getting Accepted*, Rossie Press, *Nashville, TN*
Director/Editor – *Pink Cities music video*, Western Vinyl Records, *Austin, TX*
Technical Consultant – Norman Foundation web promotion, *Chicago, IL*

201x Program Coordinator – New York State Summer School for the Arts, *Oswego, NY*
Visiting Artist Coordinator – George Simon Summer Festival, *Taos, NM*
DVD Author – *Selected Works, Oswego, NY*

200x Assistant to the Director – New York State Summer School for the Arts, *Ithaca, NY*
Web & Identity Design / Basic Coding *<www.imasample.com> Eugene, OR*
Faculty Search Committee – Cinema Production, *Eugene, OR*

PUBLICATIONS / COLLECTIONS

Sample, Ima. *Hooliganship: Playtime for the Rest of Us. (Under Review)*
Sample, Ima. "The Ceibas Cycle – A Nodal Map." *INCITE! Journal of Experimental Media & Radical Aesthetics*. Ed: B.K. Mer (201x)
"Ceibas – Sigma Fugue" (200x) available at Rocky Coast Media Library, Eugene, OR

SELECTED GRADUATE COURSEWORK

Post-Structuralist Media Theory	Experimental Film/Video	Reflexive Documentary
Emerging Practices	New Media Philosophies	Locative Media
Informatics	Documentary Ethics	Intermediation

PROFESSIONAL SKILLS

[demo reel available at www.imasample.com]

POST PRODUCTION:

Apple Final Cut	DigiDesign ProTools HD	Adobe After Effects	Apple Color
DVD Studio Pro	Cinema Tools	Apple Soundtrack Pro	Adobe Flash
Audacity	Adobe Media Encoder	Roxio Toast Titanium	FTP Clients

AUDIO PRODUCTION:
Field and Studio Recording Systems (Tascam, Marantz, Fostex, Zoom, M. Audio)

IMAGE PRODUCTION:
SD and HD Video Cameras (Panasonic HVX, Panasonic DVX, Canon XL series)

Professional Résumés for Non-faculty Positions

Let's face it. Some of you know going into this job search that you're probably better off applying for non-faculty positions in and outside the academy. You've learned that you don't like research, or that Facebook is too much of a distraction for you to get any good research done independently. You've decided that those excellent skills you've honed in your cognate area might be better suited to the private sector or private industry. Or you realize that you have so many good ideas that, unfortunately, seem to go nowhere in the academy so you're going to tap into that very un-academic entrepreneurial spirit of yours and launch your own company. Good for you. Stop apologizing right now, in the end, it doesn't matter where you land with your PhD: what matters is you've got it, so use it the right way.

The process of transforming your multi-page CV into a one to two-page résumé is less daunting than you might think. You just have to let go of a few things. There is nothing degrading about using a résumé instead of a CV. Employers outside the academic environment have different needs and expectations. All of this makes sense if you remind yourself that job-seeking documents must be appropriate to the setting and to the responsibilities of the position. Even within the academic world, certain types of positions generally call for a résumé rather than a CV. An example of this might be a position as a student services advisor or counselor. Your PhD in religion is certainly not irrelevant, but your specific teaching interests and experiences, and exact details of your scholarly activities are likely to be of lesser importance than other skills.

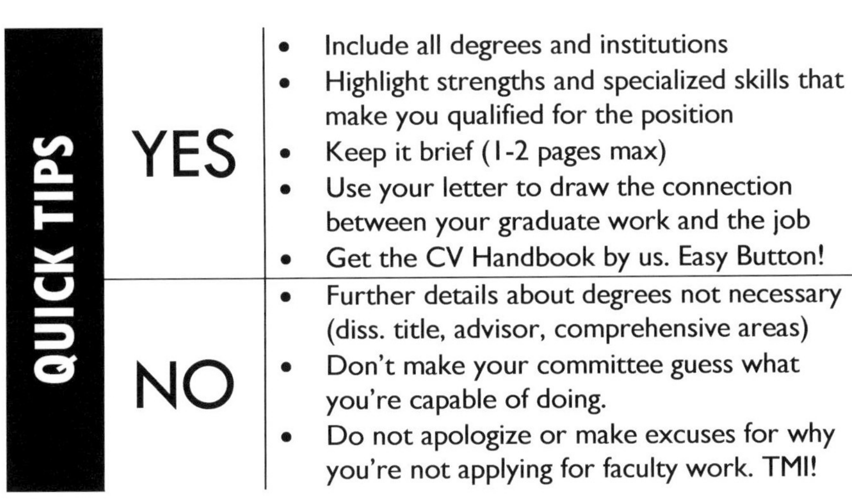

QUICK TIPS	
YES	• Include all degrees and institutions • Highlight strengths and specialized skills that make you qualified for the position • Keep it brief (1-2 pages max) • Use your letter to draw the connection between your graduate work and the job • Get the CV Handbook by us. Easy Button!
NO	• Further details about degrees not necessary (diss. title, advisor, comprehensive areas) • Don't make your committee guess what you're capable of doing. • Do not apologize or make excuses for why you're not applying for faculty work. TMI!

Sample Résumé: PhD seeking non-faculty position

Alec Example
16 University Avenue, Any City, State 12345 (101) 555-0101 a-example@gmail.com

---

COMPETENCIES Translating Writing Editing New Media

ACCOMPLISHMENTS
Proficient in Spanish, Portuguese, Swahili
Translated from Spanish to English and English to Spanish
Prepared reports for U.S. Department of Education
Created new media applications for communication
Selected as outstanding graduate teaching assistant
Awarded four-year graduate fellowship

EXPERIENCE
Language Specialist, U.S. Department of Education, 201x-present, Washington, DC

Teaching Assistant, Spanish and Portuguese Department, 201x-201x, University of Maryland

Peace Corps, Teacher Trainer and Environmental Specialist, 201x-201x, Uganda

EDUCATION
BA Biology; Spanish *with honors,* May 201x
Pacific Lutheran, Seattle, WA

MA Spanish, June 201x
University of Oregon, Eugene

PhD Second Language Acquisition, August 201x-May 201x
University of Maryland, College Park

SERVICE
Volunteer Housing Coordinator, DC Refugee Center, 201x-
Hospital Volunteer Translator, St. Mary's Hospital, 201x-
Amnesty International Board Member, 201x-201x
Animal Rescue Society (Rat Terrier), 201x

WRITING/ SPEAKING EXPERIENCES
Writing: articles published in newsletters (*Refugee Center News, Animal Rescue Read!,* and *Saving our Creatures*); managed a blog; designed brochures; developed logos; and created a nonprofit website (www.refugee_center_news.org)

Presentations: speaking engagements with local volunteer groups interested in Amnesty International projects; invited lecturer at George Washington International Center, the Peace Corps Recruitment Center, and Global Initiatives, Inc.

Writing samples available: www.alecexampleportfolio.org

Recommendations & References

Letters of recommendation and academic references continue to play an incredibly important role in the job search. It's a good idea to collect letters of recommendation early in the job search so that you are ready to go when they are called for. We notice that job seekers spend a great deal of brain power thinking about what really should be a no-brainer. We know that you're trying your hardest to simply think strategically about your letter writers: whose recommendation would be more appropriate for College A because that institution values teaching? But what about Dr. So Ahn So? Her recommendation would play particularly well to College B because that's where she began her career, but not to College C because that's where her ex teaches. STOP! You'll go crazy trying to sort out the twisted and ever-changing mess of faculty dynamics across the A-Caddy-Me. Your job is to simply put together a seamless dossier including letters that offer a coherent and consistent picture of you, the soon-to-be Rockstar Jr. faculty member.

Letters & Professional References

Letters of recommendation have been used in the academic job search since the early 1900's. Prior to FERPA in 1974, all letters of recommendation were considered confidential to the candidate. This means candidates had no access to see what others had written about them. You can imagine what a legal mess this was for colleges and universities. Following FERPA legislation, candidates had the ability to choose whether or not their letters would be confidential or open for review.

> *"When you ask me for a letter of recommendation, don't forget to say thank you; don't forget to give me a current version of your CV. Good letters take time to write."*
> ~Department Chair, Educational Measurement and Statistics

The practice of confidential letters, however, continues today; most of you probably waived your right of access to graduate school letters, and those of you in certain disciplines (most of which are in the humanities) are still strongly encouraged, primarily by your faculty, to use confidential letters of recommendation. Understand that you decide whether or not your letters are confidential. Ask your faculty advisor about the protocol in your field and follow their guidance.

While letters of recommendation have been a staple of the academic job search, search committees also request professional references (names and contact information) for folks who can speak to your academic abilities. The chair of the search will usually speak directly to your references. This makes it especially important that you share your CV not only with the folks writing your letters of recommendation, but also with your references if they are different. Most of the time, faculty advisors and other folks drafting meaningful recommendations can do so without too much assistance; however, having your CV in hand enables reference writers to provide accurate information about your experiences and speak to your potential. Unforgettable as you may be, dates and details are not always correctly recalled.

Managing your Letters of Recommendation

Collecting and managing your letters of recommendation is easy: just follow the steps and suggestions below.

Step 1: Determine how you wish to manage your letters

Individuals who plan to use letters of recommendation for employment or graduate school have two primary options with regard to managing their letters.

1) **Self-management:** You are responsible for collecting, managing, and sending your letters of recommendation. This option is recommended for the responsible graduate who's not at risk of losing, spilling coffee on, or otherwise damaging letters of recommendation. Individuals with confidential letters of recommendation cannot self-manage and must either use Interfolio or have letter writers send each letter of recommendation directly to the employer or search committee.
2) **Interfolio:** Interfolio, a higher education credentialing agency, offers a full service online letter and job-seeking document management system. Several colleges have moved their searches to Interfolio for the collection and management of all aspects of the search.

Step 2: Collect your letters

Only collect useful letters of recommendation. While you may be dying to know what Dr. So Ahn So would say about you, if you don't plan to use the letter, don't ask for it. Give letter writers specific instructions on how you would prefer to receive the letter (paper, electronic), and where they should send it (you, Interfolio, employer). Give writers ample time to compose a quality letter.

1) **Self-management:** Keep letters of recommendation in a secure place. If obtained electronically, make sure they are signed (scanned copy of signed letter or inserted .jpg signature.) More people screw this up than you would think. Save all electronic letters in a back-up location.
2) **Interfolio:** Candidates who use Interfolio can request that writers upload the letters to Interfolio directly, or can themselves upload letters to Interfolio on the writer's behalf. Writers can also submit via fax or postal mail.

Step 3: Submit your letters

Regardless of whether you self-manage your letters or use Interfolio to manage your letters, follow the specific instructions from the employer or search committee on how to submit your letters. Pay close attention to how many letters they request. Sending more (or fewer) letters than requested is considered bad etiquette.

1) **Self-management:** You should follow the specific instructions provided by the institution on submitting letters of recommendation. Pay specific attention to types (paper or electronic), number, deadlines, and request for letters from specific individuals (faculty advisor, supervisor). Make sure the letters arrive in the highest professional state possible.
2) **Interfolio:** You'll need to tell Interfolio where to send your letters of recommendation and whether the letters are to be submitted in paper or electronically.

Myths of Letters of Recommendation

There are several myths that persist about letters of recommendation and academic references. Let's first take a moment to dispel some of the more pervasive ones:

1. ***Confidential letters of recommendation are taken more seriously than non-confidential letters. Everyone should use confidential letters.***
   Confidential letters of recommendation are the gold standard in some disciplines: English, Creative Writing (well all writing for that matter), Languages, History, Religion, among others in the humanities in particular. They aren't expected or even common in some other disciplines. For the most part, your faculty will be well-aware of the expectations you face with regard to confidential/non-confidential letters of recommendations. Be sure to pay close attention to the job advertisement though, most give specific instructions for secrecy status of your letters and handling (whether they should be included in your dossier, or sent under separate cover). The realities of new online systems for managing faculty searches have actually made confidential letters quite complicated. How are you supposed to upload confidential letters of recommendation when you aren't even supposed to have the letters in the first place? You sometimes feel like saying, "My PhD is in History, Not Reference-ology!"

   Most faculty searches that still prefer or require confidential letters of recommendation have found suitable technological work-arounds, including Interfolio, which has a platform for managing faculty searches that provides for confidential letters. Visit www.interfolio.com to learn more about how Interfolio can help you manage confidential letters of recommendation. Using Interfolio whether you have confidential or non-confidential letters of recommendation is like taking an insurance policy out on your job search. It's better to lose out on a job because someone else was more qualified than because you committed a technical foul, by botching the handling of your letters or other materials in your dossier.

2. ***I need new and specific letters for each job because if the letter is tailored to the institution it will be more valuable. 'Generic' letters aren't powerful.***
   First off, let's explain what we mean when we say *generic* letters. Generic simply means that the letter isn't addressed to a specific person, position, or faculty member. It does not mean *weak* letter. We hope you are able to collect ambiguous (meaning your writer doesn't name the institution), but powerful and convincing letters of

recommendation. If your advisor is best friends with a member of a department to which you're applying, then likely your advisor will offer to write a unique letter. It would be inappropriate for you to suggest this to your advisor. Most faculty searches will elicit dozens if not hundreds of applicants as is often the case in the Humanities. Many of the doctoral students we work with apply to dozens of colleges and universities. You, and your letter writers, will go crazy trying to write that many unique letters. True, some advisors don't really change much other than the salutation and complimentary closing. Others will do more personalization.

Most of you, though, will have a single set of letters that you send to colleges and universities. If there is a compelling reason for you to request a specific detailed letter, feel empowered to do so by communicating your need clearly to your writers. Some faculty will offer to write letters that speak to different kinds of institutions. In other words, you may have a teaching letter from Doctor A and another letter from Doctor A that focuses on your research. Remember that conversation on institution type? Some faculty feel comfortable and invested in writing different letters for you. Others will balk at the suggestion that they write more than one letter. It's ok to ask a faculty member what they think of multiple letters with different emphases. You can decide if you want to go there based on their response. Using a letter service like Interfolio makes managing a search involving multiple letters much easier.

You will not need to explain this process to your faculty letter writers. They will know exactly what you mean and exactly what you want when you request a letter from them. If you have writers outside academe submitting letters on your behalf, you may need to explain to them the nuances of this particular piece of the academic job search. Their letter should be generic (meaning not addressed to a specific person or institution) but powerful meaning it highlights your strengths and experiences as a budding faculty member.

3. ***Your letters of recommendation and references should all be from tenured faculty members.***

   There once was a time when the academy was relatively homogenous: meaning most folks were tenure or tenure-track. Nowadays, the academy is a hub of professional staff and faculty. A professional staff member who is not tenured or tenure-track, may be the one to provide an excellent letter that compliments your skills as a researcher, teacher, or program coordinator. Sure, most faculty would wonder where the tenured faculty were if your dossier only included staff members, so make sure that you have a nice balance of both folks interested and knowledgeable about your academic engagement as a doctoral student and folks who may have had different contact with you on campus. Don't forget that some letters of recommendation will be expected. Take a look at the Quick Tips below for an idea of who you could include in your list of recommenders.

QUICK TIPS		
	YES	• Academic/dissertation adviser, Duh! • Examining committee member • Department faculty • Internship and practicum supervisor • Graduate teaching supervisor • Mentor • Current and previous employers (relevant only). While your talent at mixing cocktails will come in handy during the first department holiday party, your bar manager's support of your "research" skills may not be taken seriously.
	NO	• Graduate students in your department who can speak to your collegiality. This is a quick kiss of death. • Undergraduate or graduate students whom you taught. You might include positive teaching comments in a teaching portfolio but letters from students are considered nonsensical. • A relative in the same field. Get real.

They are so critical, in fact, that many job seekers miss out on some job-search bonus points because they've either selected the wrong folks to write references or they somehow manage to botch the process.

Sharing your Letters of Recommendation

Sharing your letters of recommendation shouldn't be complicated, but man, people really screw this step up. Take a look at this quick guide that summarizes the process.

1 Follow Instructions for Submission

- It's not that hard, really, to just follow instructions; search committees and others rely on you to do just that. If they want three recommendations, send or upload three. This really goes for all types of applications, but sometimes with email/online processes, people can get kind of carried away or informal.
- Upload documents with recognizable file names. (e.g. Drsmithletter.pdf)

2 Share only PDFs of your Documents

- When search committees open your Word document, anything might show up with a green or red squiggly line. Those red and green lines send messages to your brain – ERROR! Your letters of recommendation are official documents. That's right: keep your hands off them. You cannot edit or fix typos on them. Send only as pdfs, that way if Dr. So Ahn So misspelled something or used sentence fragments, you won't get the blame and your committee may not notice.

3 Skip Steps 1 & 2 and Just Use Interfolio

- We don't know why this happens, but folks really get nervous when they apply online: maybe it's that lack of seeing the Postmaster throw your letter into the mail bag. Interfolio manages your applications for you, so all you need to do is tell them where to send your materials (all of them, even your confidential letters). They put together a nice looking and professional dossier, even with a table of contents. Wow, you're an author.
- Save headaches, save trees, save your marriage, and use Interfolio.

Additionally, be sure to give your writers plenty of notice, and thank them for taking the time to write a complimentary letter on your behalf. Your academic network includes those who'll help you advance to the next level. Never take them for granted.

21st Century Communication

No. You may not friend, poke or tweet to or about members of your search committee or others involved with your academic job search. Does it sound like you're being scolded? Sorry. That's not our intention, but we are absolutely amazed at how few boundaries people seem to have these days. We get it, you're desperate for a job, but cyber-stalking the chair of the search committee and friending and poking him on Facebook is not going to win you points with the search committee nor does it "demonstrate technology integration" nor does it demonstrate "a go get it" attitude. Mostly, it just demonstrates sheer desperation and professional naiveté, otherwise known as AWKWARD.

Effective communication via the written word (shared electronically or on paper) is a fundamental, universal, and critical step in any job search. It's also the place where many job seekers stumble or fumble the ball. All of this is complicated by the 21st century laissez-faire approach to formal communication. We've become accustomed, even in work settings, to abbreviated, terse, quick and often informal communication patterns. The job search requires attention to this particular issue in ways that are attuned to the new patterns of communication, but that adhere to, perhaps, more traditional modes of communication. Academe, and those who rule, it still prefer and expect a bit of formality in this process. Think this way: WTF: Write Things Formally. Or OMG: Official, Meaningful, Grammatical. BTW: search committees care about this, so take it seriously.

> *"Letters give voice to your dossier. We're looking at your entire package and evaluating: can this person really do this? Are they a writer? Do they understand professionalism? Can they communicate well? We have lots of constituents who care deeply about these things: from our students, to our alumni, to our grant partners, to our donors. We need someone with a sense of how to communicate on paper, in person, and online. We look at all three modalities."*
>
> ~Assistant Dean, Business College

We know you're busy, but one other critical factor with respect to job-search communication is that there's no time to delay. Everything is time sensitive, from getting off your butt to write your cover letter, to responding to the Chair's phone message that they'd like to offer you the job. There's no excuse or reason to procrastinate, or even avoid communication. You might miss out on a job opportunity if you don't treat every aspect of your job search as time sensitive. Most candidates procrastinate because they think they don't know what to say. Most job seekers think only of writing letters of application, but many other letters and kinds of correspondence will occur during the job search. Each should be approached with an awareness of its unique function and importance. It's nearly impossible to prepare you for each potential interaction you'll have with a search committee so here are some communication conventions followed by more detailed information about a few of the gold standards in the academic job search: the cover letter, the thank you letter, the contract letters.

QUICK TIPS		
	YES	• Know the context for the communication. Even short emails should be formally written and always include a formal salutation and a complimentary closing. • If leaving a voicemail, be sure to articulately pronounce your name and return phone number. • Thank you notes are always appreciated, even when sent in an email. • Signed contracts should be sent via certified mail or scanned and sent as a high resolution pdf.
	NO	• Avoid informal contact over Facebook. Even liking the department that you're about to visit might be a little much. • Avoid emoticons in emails or other written correspondance until after you've gotten tenure. By then you'll be too lazy. • Don't CC or BCC people who aren't involved in the job search. It's weird to CC your advisor on negotiations with a search committee – that just looks co-dependant. • Don't discuss your job search over Facebook, twitter or other social media outlet. Chances are someone will know you're communicating about them.

Cover Letters

Perhaps nothing is more complicated to most job seekers than writing an effective cover letter. Why? It probably has something to do with how beaten down you feel by the time you reach that stage of your academic job search combined with the knowledge you possess that the job market for tenure-track positions will once again be abysmal this year coupled with the tremendous burden of the excessive student loans you took out to afford that studio apartment and the excessive "study" trips to Rome. Breathe. It's time to pause and remember something. You can do this. You've done it for the last several years. Nothing can possibly be as bad, by the way, as that intermediate statistics course. You are capable, beautiful, and qualified to do this work. So quit whining and let's get to the work of creating a meaningful cover letter.

How to begin your cover letter is often the most difficult part of the process. Let's break it down and see the cover letter, at least in the beginning, as pieces of your credential that you'll market to employers versus seeing it, at least for now, as one unified whole. OK. This is not anatomy 101. Your letters do have form, much like the human body. Your job is to make it look like it has form, to make it appear like it fits together. So what are the basic parts of a cover letter and what matters most in each? Take a look at the following sections to learn how to draft a meaningful and thus targeted cover letter.

Salutation

Developing a targeted letter begins with the inside address and the salutation. Whenever possible, address the letter to a specific person, using full name and exact title. Most search advertisements include the name of the search chair. We often get asked, "To whom should I address the letter when nobody specifically is listed?" Well, you've just spent the last five or more years learning how to be a good researcher, this includes having learned the ability to make informed decisions. Be empowered to pick up the phone or log onto the internet to locate more details about the specific search. When no specific name is given, or a generic, "Search Committee" for a specific search or department is listed, don't fret. Simply follow the specific instructions and use the simplified style of a business letter which omits both the salutation and complimentary closing.

Don't underestimate the importance of the salutation: it offers more opportunity for error than any other part of your letter. Frequently used but not recommended salutations such as *Dear Head*, and *Dear Sir,* amuse some professionals, offend others, and impress none. Remember, *no* dead-end dears. The list is long but here are a few common ones:

- Dear Chair
- Dear Faculty
- Dear Person
- Dear Friends
- Dear People
- Dear Head
- Dear Reader
- Dear Colleague
- Dear Sir
- Dear Ladies
- To Whom it may concern
- Mesdames
- Gentlemen
- Dear Friends and Colleagues
- Hello
- Good day

And so we don't forget, salutations are followed by a colon (:) not a comma (,).

Introduction

It's important in the first few lines of your letter to establish a connection between you and the search committee. One of the most common errors of the novice job seeker is coming on too strong in the first paragraph and telling the search committee to suspend their search because they've found the perfect candidate in you. While you do want to work to convince them of this, understand your onslaught should last over an entire letter, not just in the first paragraph. How many first dates are ruined when one person tries to make the first move too quickly?

Avoid ambiguity. In order for your letter to receive proper handling and attention, the first paragraph must state clearly the exact title of the position for which you wish to be considered as a candidate. It is also a good idea to let the reader know how you learned of the opening. For example:

> *I am writing in response to the position announcement for an Assistant Professor in the School of Behavioral Sciences at Big State posted in the September 18th edition of the Chronicle of Higher Education (job #327265).*

Once you've made it clear for which position you're applying, gently introduce yourself and position your credentials in both your current department where most of you are completing your degree and in their department where you hope to make your degree work.

> *My Ph.D. will be conferred from Big State University in May 201x. As a doctoral student at a comparable research institution, I've been engaged in a wide variety of professional opportunities as a researcher, teacher, and committed member of the community. While I will elaborate on each of these areas in greater detail, my interest in your department, in short, stems from what I perceive to be a parallel focus based on my knowledge of your faculty and departmental outreach efforts.*

In this short paragraph the writer has indicated degree status (Are you even in the running for this job?) and also indicated that the degree was from a comparable institution. It's nice to highlight your experience working in digs like theirs. The writer highlights commonalities as a scholar, teacher, and active member of the community and then, immediately notes that the hiring department also seems to be engaged in similar pursuits. Oh, and lastly, the writer states something that each opening paragraph must state: I want to work for you!

Body

While the body of your letter is considerably longer than the opening paragraph, we find it substantially easier to compose; you're writing your own autobiography (just watch the length). While most of you probably learned that modesty is a virtue, it's time to bare it all on your cover letter. Don't worry about being modest but don't go overboard and come off as an ego-maniac. Remember, big-name tenured faculty will be reading this and, like the Honey Badger, they won't really care how self-important you are; they can read you like a book. (YouTube: Honey Badger for inspiration.)

The body of the letter consists of several paragraphs highlighting your qualifications. Lead off with the most substantial or significant elements of your academic identity. If you are a researcher, jump right into your dissertation research and emphasize elements of your research identity that are highly marketable. Hopefully, you've launched a dissertation that is both meaningful and marketable given your profession's current discussions. Take a look at the following topics that any budding researcher will address in a cover letter:

• *Research Interests*	• *Supervised Research Projects*
• *Dissertation & Methodology*	• *Grants and Funding*
• *Topical Summary of Publications*	• *Presentations on Research*
• *Statistical/Research Software*	• *Significant Mentors*
• *Lab Experience & Protocol*	• *Awards & Honors in Research Area*
• *Workshops in Research Area*	• *Public Outreach in Research Area*
• *Future Directions of Research*	• *Research Applications (outside Academe)*

If you are marketing yourself as a teacher, it's still not a bad idea to lead off with the dissertation. You, like most folks in the midst of their dissertation, will be completely engrossed in the process and likely have a lot to say about it (even if it involves the occasional four letter word). Then, clearly you'll want to highlight your expertise as a teacher. As a teacher-scholar be sure to address the following in your cover letter:

• *Teaching Assistantships*	• *Courses Taught*
• *Teaching Philosophy*	• *Technology Integration in Teaching*
• *Teaching Responsibilities*	• *Teaching Interests*
• *Teaching Awards and Honors*	• *Student Assessment & Evaluation*
• *Teaching Fellowships*	• *Student Engagement*
• *Student Satisfaction/Motivation*	• *Invited Speakers/Guests*
• *Future Teaching Interests*	• *Master Classes*

Lastly, the body of your cover letter should address the ways in which you engage in both your profession and the community and how your particular line of expertise is relevant in today's world. You probably addressed some of this already, but it's a good idea to revisit and remind those reading your materials what a good colleague, student mentor, and member of the professoriate you'll be. Jr. faculty members are often asked to participate in their share of departmental committees and may have responsibilities outside of the department even as they work toward tenure. Knowledge of the institution to which you're applying will help you determine the extent to which you need to highlight your ability to serve the institution and its mission by participating in institutional service obligations. The following list includes some areas that are often nice bonuses for search committees. Don't forget to include or address them.

• *Campus Leadership*	• *Advising Experience*
• *Committee Leadership*	• *Collaborative Projects*
• *Graduate Student Engagement*	• *Volunteer Service to the Profession*
• *Student Group Involvement*	• *Professional Development*
• *Mentoring Programs*	• *Professional Service*
• *Events Organized/Developed*	• *Institutional/Departmental Outreach*
• *Active Affiliations*	• *Community Volunteer Experience*

Take some time to read and reread the position announcement carefully. Remember the discussion from earlier in the book? Your cover letter is an opportunity for you to use your excellent writing skills (no one gets this far without being able to write decently) to align your experiences with the search committee's needs. Concentrate on experiences related to the duties and responsibilities presented in the position announcement. Refer to your CV and expand upon relevant items. Emphasize the positive and ignore the weak areas. Do not apologize for not meeting the "exact" qualifications requested, in fact don't even bring them up. Most search committees would prefer to read concise letters that run about two pages in length. Your paragraphs should:

- Grab the reader's attention with a significant accomplishment or two (awards, funding, publications). *Why are you interesting?*
- Talk about who you are as a teacher, researcher, and potential colleague. *What is the importance of your research?*
- This is a good place to drop names of key faculty, key organizations and commissions, and collaborating institutions. By adding this information, you divulge details about your ability to collaborate and further enhance your credential as an up-an-coming scholar. *Who do you know?*
- Talk about your teaching and the impact your style has had on the students and their learning success. Highlight your strengths: like integrating technology in a learning environment or working with students and faculty in collaborative settings. *What can you do for our students?*
- Weave in the basic tenets of your philosophy. It will certainly set you apart from other candidates who do not take the time to demonstrate how their beliefs influence their practice. *How will we see your philosophy in action?*

Can the reader still hear your voice? If it sounds like a form letter, start over! It's true. Most letters are dreadfully dull because writers don't give it any voice. Don't be one of those, and don't be afraid to give yourself some time. Most really well-written letters take time, sometimes more time than updating a CV. Share your letter with others, especially your faculty, but be prepared for their feedback and be prepared to go back to the drawing board or the coffee house.

Conclusion

The main thrust of a concluding paragraph should be your interest in discussing the position and your qualifications more fully in an interview. In the final paragraph of your cover letter indicate that you've concluded your tasks regarding their search requests (that supporting documents are available, enclosed, uploaded, attached). It's not the time to indicate that you'll *soon* be getting to upload, send, or submit any materials. You must have this completed and indicate that, to your knowledge, all materials have now been successfully submitted. It's not a bad idea to call and verify that the department has received everything but it's also potentially an annoyance. You don't want the departmental secretary mentioning you were confused about whether your materials had been uploaded successfully. Most online application portals send applicants messages or give updates on the status of uploaded documents.

It goes without saying that this final paragraph should include a note of thanks for the search committee's time in your consideration. Indicate any plans you may have to attend a national meeting where they might be conducting screening interviews. It's a cheap way for the search committee to get a sense of who you are. If you're giving a presentation, this is an excellent opportunity to invite the search committee. They get a chance to meet you and learn about your research and see your presentation style. It's a win all around for them.

Avoid stating that you are the "perfect candidate."

There may be someone, somewhere, who is capable of writing a humorous letter of application successfully, but most attempts fail, and fail badly. A sense of humor is a wonderful gift but you will have opportunities to display your wit and cleverness at a later stage of the selection process. Be cautious of any variation from standard, formal communication in either style or format. Anything other than a fairly straightforward application letter tends to smack of desperation. Regardless of the length of the letter, proof the contents and check your letter for action, much like you did for your CV. Examine your sentences and see if you have used a variety of action verbs, like the ones below:

Accomplished	Advised	Authored	Chaired	Collaborated
Collected	Coordinated	Created	Designed	Developed
Elected	Engineered	Established	Facilitated	Generated
Instructed	Investigated	Managed	Motivated	Negotiated
Organized	Participated	Preformed	Prepared	Podcasted
Represented	Researched	Restructured	Served	Shaped
Streamlined	Supervised	Taught	Trained	Volunteered

Most job seekers breathe a huge sigh of relief once that dossier gets out the door. Your work and potential communication don't stop here, though. Too many job seekers end up making a poor or unprofessional impression because they fail to fine tune their communication style to mesh with the professional expectation of the academy. You may find the following occasions where professional communication is expected and could even be what seals the deal for you in the end, so pay attention.

Requests for Additional Materials

After the initial application has been made with an employer, you may be asked to provide additional samples or information. Woohoo! Is what you should be thinking. This is a great sign that a search committee is so interested in you that they'd like to learn more. They might ask for samples of your work including writing samples, dissertation abstracts, syllabi, teaching evaluations, performance CDs/DVDs, slides of artwork or coaching films. All additional materials sent to the search committee should be accompanied by a letter or email that offers thanks for the opportunity to share additional details and that also outlines the contents of the enclosures or attachments. Most online application portals have very specific and easy-to-use uploading procedures for required search documents. You may notice, after receiving a request for additional materials, that new prompts exist to upload specific materials. Pay careful attention that the correct file is uploaded to the correct category.

Thank You Letters

Thank you, thank you, thank you. Politicians, movie stars, comedians each seem to have their own special way of saying thanks. It's time for you to develop yours. These two little words can go a long way in impressing your search committee and others to whom you should offer thanks. It's overkill to send Hallmarks to everyone who took the time to speak to you while on your campus visit, but all too often only one person gets the thank you, the search chair. It's important in that letter if you choose to send only one, to request that they share your thanks with members of the search committee and others who played a key role during your campus visit.

In addition to being a professional courtesy, a follow-up letter gives you, the candidate, one more chance to reemphasize important components of the interview. It is always appropriate to express continued interest in the position. If, following the campus visit, you realize there's no way in hell you'd work at that dump, don't withdraw from consideration in a thank you letter. It's best to pick up the phone or send a professional email thanking them for the courtesy but offering your regrets on having to remove your name from consideration. It's still a good idea to do all of this with the highest level of professionalism and sincere gratitude. If you are required to submit paperwork to have any portion of the travel expenses reimbursed, be sure to say thanks first and conclude with the business. Rushing into reimbursement before properly thanking those involved in your visit makes you look self-absorbed and unsophisticated.

Accepting & Rejecting Offers

When you receive an offer but are not able to make an immediate decision to accept or decline, a letter acknowledging the receipt of the offer or contract should be sent promptly. The employer typically requests your decision within a certain time period. If you anticipate that you will not be able to reach a decision within the specified time, you may use this letter or email communication to request a reasonable extension. A delay of this type is not routine and should only be used in exceptional circumstances. Most often a decision to accept or reject a contract can be reached without resorting to this type of communication.

If you have decided to accept an offer received in person, by telephone, email or letter, your acceptance should be stated in writing, recorded in an email, or both. If a formal contract is offered, it should be signed and returned with a brief cover letter. If there is no formal contract, the letter of acceptance should clearly state the terms of the appointment including title of position, salary, and starting date. If the appointment is for a fixed term, the duration should be stated.

If you have decided to decline an offer, a communication indicating your decision must be sent promptly. A verbal refusal should be confirmed in writing. It is always a good idea to express appreciation for the offer. You are not obligated to explain your decision for refusing the offer. As a professional, you want your letter to reflect tact and courtesy. Remember, it is a small world and future employment possibilities could be affected.

Focus your Letter

The cover letter provides an excellent opportunity to not only express your interest in the position but to explain how your academic background and skills-set fits the opening. While most of us are a bit shy about promoting ourselves, the cover letter is based on facts and past experiences. And, it doesn't reveal any blushing!

> *"The biggest mistake candidates make in a cover letter is sounding too vague and unbelievable because they think we always want a self-starter with real passion. Look, I want someone who can tell me definitively about something specific they've done and why that experience will help them be successful at Big State University. I believe them when it's real."*
>
> ~ Professor, Music

Quality counts: It's not unusual for employers to comment about the quality, *or lack of quality*, of job-search communications. Taking the time to write a well-crafted letter will pay off as this becomes your outline for future letters. There is no doubt that a meaningful and focused cover letter will set you apart from other job seekers. We are always amazed at how many typos and other grammatical errors make it to the chair's desk in a cover letter. In this day and age, the competition is too fierce to overlook the minor details like proofing your documents. A well written, clean and clear letter is critical. If they find a typo, especially if it's obvious the reader didn't proof the letter, sorry Charlie, you usually end up in my recycle bin. Ugh!"

> *"Tell me why you are the best candidate for the job. Don't forget the purpose of a cover letter is to market skills, abilities, and potential."*
>
> ~Department Head, Journalism

LETTER CHECKUP CHECKLIST

☐	Business format	☐	White paper (if sending by post)
☐	Review salutation (no dead-end dears!)	☐	Address letter to proper individual (have you used the right title?)
☐	Avoid the overuse of the pronoun "I"	☐	Check the opening of each paragraph: do they capture the reader's attention?
☐	Font should match CV and other materials in dossier	☐	Check your spelling
☐	Even margins (1")	☐	Check your grammar
☐	Provide page numbers after the first page of your letter	☐	Match job advertisement duties with your skills and experiences
☐	Incorporate your teaching philosophy	☐	Share relevant points of your dissertation
☐	Avoid including personal information or license/certificate numbers in letter	☐	Saved as pdf
☐	Completely accurate and factual information in the letter	☐	Does it read like a form letter? Start over.
☐	Keep a copy for your records	☐	One last time, Spellcheck! Proof!

Sample Letter with key call-outs—know why you are writing!

[Return Address]
Your Street Address
Your City, State, Zip Code
Date

[Inside Address]
Committee Chair: Person, Title
Department: Name of Department
Institution: Name of University/Organization
Address: Street Address, City, State, Zip Code

[Salutation]
Dear Dr. Sample:

[Opening paragraph]

Institutions could have numerous openings, so make a clear statement about why you are writing.

[Body paragraphs]

Point out in the body of the letter specific qualifications and experiences directly related to the position. Emphasize appropriate training and incorporate brief statements about your teaching/research experiences, philosophy or research agendas, and any special experiences that relate to this position or the institution. The body of the letter allows you to sell yourself as someone competent and ready to be part of an academic unit.

[Concluding paragraph]

End your letter by including a reference to the next step in the process, the interview.

[Complimentary Closing]

Sincerely,
(Your Signature)
Type Your Name
Enclosures: Curriculum Vitae, Teaching Portfolio, Writing Sample

Sample Cover Letter

111 College Street
Any Town, Any State 12345
March 1, 201x

So Ahn So, Ph.D.
Big 10 State University
School of Behavioral Sciences
90123 Main Street
Any City, Any State 12345

Dear Dr. So Ahn So:

I am writing in response to the position announcement for an Assistant Professor of Rehabilitation Counseling Education (tenure track) in the School of Behavioral Sciences at Big 10 State posted in the September 18th edition of the Chronicle of Higher Education. I will receive my Ph.D. in Rehabilitation Counseling from The Big State University in May of 201x. As a doctoral student at a comparable research institution, I have commensurate experience as an emerging scholar with the tripartite mission of a large state school like yours. My background in special education and rehabilitation counseling has anchored my research, teaching and service to encourage genuine results for the individuals our discipline strives to serve. Likewise, the Professional Code of Ethics for Rehabilitation Counselors has guided my professionalism, community service, and advocacy efforts within our field.

As a doctoral candidate, I recently received funding from the National Center for Rehabilitation Counseling to complete my dissertation, entitled, "Bridging the gap: Generational, Racial, and Gender Differences in the Rehabilitation Process." In my dissertation, I examine the provision of rehabilitative services over the last 30 years and note a variety of political, economic, and social variables and the effects these variables have had on the individuals receiving services and the organizations providing those services. The study also draws on my international experience as a special education teacher in the United Arab Emirates to examine patterns in international policy and the provision of services for individuals with disabilities. This international research, partially funded by the US Commission on International Educational Policy (USCIEP), has also appeared in two publications that I coauthored with advising faculty members from Big State University, United Arab Emirates University in Al Ain, and the Humboldt University in Berlin. My collaborative research efforts have led to beneficial emerging partnerships between three major international universities.

My teaching experience spans two continents and two decades. As a special education teacher in the US and United Arab Emirates, I worked closely with children and their families on developing appropriate learning and lifeskills plans. These plans ranged from developmentally ready knowledge to lifeskills like personal care, daily living skills, and employment skills to ensure the highest level of individual independence and quality of life. As an employment facilitator for young adults, I sought community partnerships throughout the business sector and public agencies to maximize utilization of public resources while also maximizing an individual's potential for self-directed success. This practical experience has informed my college teaching, where I teach adults the necessary skills to be effective rehabilitation counselors in their respective areas of expertise.

Sample Cover Letter, page 2

Will B. Goode, Page 2

In addition to my accomplishments as a researcher and teacher, I have actively participated in multiple service engagements throughout the university community, locally and abroad. As a board member for Community Health Alliance, I oversaw the implementation of a new community outreach program geared at the early diagnoses of developmental disabilities to provide earlier interventions for needy families. In my role as a teaching assistant at Big State University, I also led several organizations and organized multiple professional meetings and programs for undergraduate and graduate students. As the Graduate Student Ambassador to the Rehabilitation Counseling Association (RCA), I also worked on the newly updated Professional Code of Ethics on Faculty-Student professional relationships. I have reviewed several materials for publication, and those reviews appear in multiple journals and online list-serves. More detailed information about my work as a reviewer can be found in my CV. While in the UAE, I volunteered my services as a consultant during the implementation of a new data tracking and management system used by case workers to track goals and outcomes for individuals with disabilities served throughout the UAE. This system and the positive outcomes it supported has been adopted elsewhere.

My teaching philosophy, which is included with this letter, holds that all individuals with the necessary supports can achieve their maximum potential regardless of their barriers. This is my guiding philosophy not only when I work with students and adults with disabilities, but also when I work with emerging graduate students. I work to provide students the support that they need as their professional identities emerge. I've gained valuable insight into this process while serving on the mentoring committee for new graduate students and assisting with the new faculty orientation for the Counseling Rehabilitation Program while at Big State University. I twice served on a search committee for new faculty in our program area on invitation from the Dean. This process has given me great insight into the inner workings of academe while also providing me with practical experience in the mentoring process for both new graduate students and tenure-track faculty.

As the application materials stated, I have enclosed my curriculum vitae, sample of scholarly writing, and teaching philosophy with this material. My ePortfolio also contains a number of resources including my complete teaching portfolio, expanded research agenda and comprehensive listing of my service activities. Additionally, my complete list of publications and presentations are also linked for your further review. My background in rehabilitation counseling, coupled with my expertise in technology, international experience, and professional qualifications uniquely match what I perceive to be the requirements for this position. I would welcome the opportunity to discuss this position in detail with you and I will be happy to arrange a time to interview with you at your convenience. Thank you for your consideration, and if you require additional information, please contact me directly.

Sincerely,

Will Goode

Will B. Goode

Enclosures

Sample Cover Letter: Position Outside Academe

211College Street
Any Place, State Zip
March 1, 201x

I.M. Boss, Ph.D.
CTS Solutions
90123 Main Street
Any City, Any State 12345

Dear Dr. Boss:

I am writing in response to the position opening of Assistant Director of Computer Testing Research (#321321-4) at Computerized Testing Solutions which is posted on your website. I will receive my doctorate from Big State University in Educational Measurement in May. My dissertation defense is scheduled for April 11, 201x. This letter, along with the various other application materials requested by CTS, will provide details on my graduate studies and my previous professional and educational experiences.

My advanced coursework directly relates to the demands of the position including applied statistics, psychometric and statistical procedures, testing theory and test development. Under the guidance of faculty, I authored two articles on computer-mediated testing. In addition to my publications, I have been an active presenter at state, national and international meetings in the field of computerized testing. While at Big State, I have also had the privilege of working with and conducting research on behalf of the National Testing Programs, the group responsible for the Integrated Basic Skills Examination. This position provided me the opportunity to refine my skills while working with a number of variables involved in the administration, scoring, and validating of such a large-scale test.

Over the last two summers I interned at CT Inc., where I conducted analyses for two researchers involved with the CT college entrance exam. In this position, I developed my skills in testing theories and their practical application. While at CT Inc., I worked in a collaborative environment further refining my skills as a team player through goal planning, project mapping, and resource utilization. Additionally, I was able to further study issues related to designing, developing, and validating computer/web-based tests. I successfully implemented technology to drive product advancement, while balancing the delicate needs of information management in this digital age.

I would welcome the opportunity to discuss this position in detail with you and I will be happy to arrange a time to interview with you at your convenience. As your website instructed, I have submitted the online employment application, uploaded three letters of recommendation as well as my CV. Thank you for your consideration.

Sincerely,

Cat N Méasure

Cat N. Méasure

Thank You Letter: Post-Interview

211College Street
Any Place, State Zip
March 1, 201x

So Ahn So, Ph.D.
Big State University
School of Behavioral Sciences
90123 Main Street
Any City, Any State 12345

Dear Dr. So Ahn So:

With gratitude, I am writing to thank you for a very meaningful and exhilarating campus visit on January 12-13, 201x. Meeting your faculty, talking to your staff, and interacting with the graduate students was most satisfying. You had shared with me in earlier conversations that you had a unique situation in your department and I certainly left the interview with that thought in mind. The assistant professor position remains very attractive to me and I feel that with my background in quantitative analysis and my recent teaching assistantships, I could join your department and be an active member from the very beginning.

The graduate students asked me two questions that I think are most valuable: "What can you do for us as busy and anxious graduate students?" "What can you bring to us and our programs?" I responded to them that I understood their realities and would be prepared to make each class meaningful and engaging. During my Graduate Teaching Certificate coursework and practicum, I was mentored by a professor who was a master at motivating students. He taught me the importance of developing a philosophy and of practicing that philosophy in every academic endeavor. He encouraged me to use my strengths as a researcher to help teach students about the relationship between the research and the application of their work.

Again, let me reiterate my interest in the position. If additional materials are needed or should you or any others involved in the interview process have questions for me, please feel free to contact me via email, Skype or phone. Thank you.

Sincerely,

Will Goode

Will B. Goode

Rejection Letter

211 College Street
Any Place, Any State Zip
March 1, 201x

I.M. Boss, Ph.D.
Big State University
School of Religion
90123 Main Street
Any City, Any State 12345

Dear Dr. Boss:

First, let me share with you my deepest appreciation for extending to me the Assistant Professor offer in ABC's Religion Department. Having the opportunity to speak at length with you about the teaching and research opportunities at Big State University, the offer was most gratifying. It is with regret that circumstances do not allow me to accept your offer at this time.

Again, I want to share with you my appreciation for being considered for this position. I do hope that I will have the opportunity to interact with you in professional meetings in the near future and perhaps work on funding opportunities that we discussed. In the meantime, I want to wish you and your department all the best.

Sincerely,

Bea Goode

Bea Goode

Acceptance Letter

211 College Street
Any Place, Any State Zip
March 1, 201x

Ima Smart, Dean
Big State University
College of Arts and Sciences
90123 Main Street
Any City, Any State 12345

Dear Dean Smart:

I received both the email and offer letter from you today, March 24, 201x. As you know, the offer is most gratifying and I accept the tenure-track position of Assistant professor (#2819181) in the College of Arts and Sciences to begin August 1, 201x. I am fully aware of the research and teaching responsibilities I am accepting with this position and am deeply honored by the confidence you have placed in me.

Enclosed with this letter, please find the official job offer with my signature. I look forward to future communications with you.

Sincerely,

Bea Goode

Bea Goode
Enclosures

Keeping Good Records

Most job seekers will have multiple applications out when they are on the market. Keep a log to track your communications with various institutions. You might go crazy trying to remember names, dates, all the while writing your dissertation. Use this letter log to track all communications between you and a specific search.

Job title:
Institution:
Date applied/application uploaded:
Follow-up communications:

Job title:
Institution:
Date applied/application uploaded:
Follow-up communications:

Job title:
Institution:
Date applied/application uploaded:
Follow-up communications:

Job title:
Institution:
Date applied/application uploaded:
Follow-up communications:

Philosophy Statements

It would be a crying shame if you left your doc program unable to articulate your vision for teaching and research. We call these grandiose statements philosophy statements. Of course, we act as though we never stray from these impressive and lofty ideas about teaching (mostly) and research (called research statements). When in reality, we know that we use our philosophies and statements as a guide, a compass of sorts, and hope that we at least come close to hitting the mark. If your philosophy really does guide your work (and it should) and your philosophy is grounded in relatively informed research and best practices in pedagogy in your field, you should be in a good position.

Teaching Philosophy

The struggle that most job seekers have is: 1) they fail to have a completely articulate and rehearsed statement about their teaching practice that they support with solid classroom experiences; or 2) they miss the mark when it comes to addressing some key transformations in the way we interact with students in the academy (including technology, differentiating instruction to make it accessible to all students, and presenting a culturally fair and non-biased curriculum).

Chances are that you were asked to submit a philosophy statement as you applied to your graduate program. Of course, this statement likely addressed your personal or early career goals and may not address teaching at all. But if you feel like you're starting from scratch, try to find this document to help you get started. It worked to get you into the graduate program, right? Most of you were probably also asked to submit your teaching philosophy or at least to verbally address it as you interviewed for teaching assistantships. If you were never asked to articulate this on paper, it's time to get writing.

A common mistake made by many doc students is thinking that their teaching philosophy statement is a summary of their CV. Wrong! A teaching philosophy is an outline of your beliefs and your values about teaching and learning with supported classroom experiences and examples. It's more than a broad philosophical statement. They want examples. If you believe in the meaningful integration of technology, tell us what that looks like in your classroom. If you value diversity and cultural competency, how do you realize that in your classes or interactions with students? You might be thinking, *But we don't talk about those things in my Freshmen Chemistry lectures?* We wonder, why not? Certainly your chemistry lecture or discussion section is full of students from diverse backgrounds, racial and ethnic identities, sexualities, socio-economic backgrounds. All of these variables are at work in your classroom. How do you tell them that you value their diverse experiences? How do they know that you recognize how diversity can shape classroom learning and university experiences? (We mean more than just a statement in a syllabus.)

Use the following list to reflect on the teaching and learning experiences that have shaped your identity as a teacher and a student. Try to locate examples from your experiences as both a student and teacher. The following topics permeate most learning environments:

- *Theories of Learning*
- *Formative Assessment*
- *Summative Assessment*
- *Syllabus Design*
- *Grading Policies*
- *Diversity/Equity Issues*
- *Student Evaluations*
- *Service Learning/Unique Learning*
- *Course Management Systems*
- *Learning Styles and Preferences*
- *Assignments*
- *Support Outside of Class*
- *Mentoring*
- *Technology Integration*

Members of search committees often consider the philosophy statement to be as important as the CV. Why? Your philosophy statement (both written and orally rehearsed) should be able to answer the following questions:

- Why do you want to teach?
- What makes you an effective teacher?
- What beliefs, methods, and theories influence your teaching?
- How do you motivate students to learn?
- How do you evaluate student work and learning?
- How do you know students are effectively learning the material before an end of term assessment (formative assessment)?
- How do you assess and improve your own teaching?
- What elements of your research will be evident in your teaching?
- How does student feedback influence your teaching practices?
- How do you use technology to facilitate learning? What technologies?

The more thorough the statement, the better picture you paint of your notions of teaching and learning. Like all good job seeking materials, your philosophy statement should be a concise, honest reflection of your professional beliefs and objectives and, of course, free of errors of grammar or usage. Most search committees will ask you to submit a one or two-page teaching philosophy. Like any academic submission, the paper should be titled and include your name on all pages. Use the same font that you have chosen for your application letters and CV. That's easy and communicates that you understand the importance of image and design.

Your teaching philosophy should follow you into your first teaching position, first year review, and even to your final bid for tenure.

Ask any newly hired assistant professor. Those that put together a well-written essay about their philosophy during their graduate studies will thank the stars that they have it for their first-year review.

> *"Moving, getting settled, starting a new course, adjusting in my new role as an assistant professor—it's overwhelming! I felt confident about the teaching philosophy I used to find this job and with just a minor tweak or two, could add it to my first-year review materials."*
>
> ~Assistant Professor

Sure, the teaching philosophy is commonly requested of most job seekers, but it comes as a surprise to many first-year faculty that the teaching philosophy is a key document in their promotion and tenure dossier. If you have it in your ePortfolio, you'll be well on your way to a positive first-year review.

Writing a Research Statement

Much like a teaching philosophy, a research statement conveys your research interests in your academic specialty, defines your particular research in very specific terms, and situates it within your field. Additionally, your statement communicates the passion you hold for your niche-research area. Hiring committees from research-based institutions find this document to be an essential piece of the academic job-search dossier.

Your research statement is a valuable tool that promotes your candidacy if it:

- Demonstrates an active and well-defined research plan;
- Shows promise for securing external funding and support;
- Validates research knowledge and capability, particularly as it relates to the hiring department, college, or university;
- Positions you to become the crème de la crème of your field;
- Clearly identifies strategic partners, collaborators, and individuals in your area that would be promising for your department;
- Communicates ways in which you plan to involve students both at the undergraduate and graduate level;
- Articulates future research goals, directions, and benefits to the field, society, and perhaps even the department's coffers.

Use the following list to reflect on the research and lab experiences that have shaped your identity as a researcher. The following topics are relevant in discussions of research experiences:

• *Research Coursework*	• *Lab Protocols*
• *Methodologies*	• *Human Subject Review Boards*
• *Statistical Analysis Experience*	• *Research Databases*
• *Statistical Software*	• *Primary Journals in Your Field*
• *Quantitative Methods*	• *Presentations (Posters, Talks)*
• *Qualitative Methods*	• *Supervised Research*
• *Research Ethics*	• *Literature Reviews*

Writing a research statement is pretty straight forward. Chances are you'll write mostly about your dissertation or other culminating process that led to the granting of your terminal degree. While most fellow docs are appreciative and even sympathetic to the process of writing a thesis, they are usually not that interested in hearing what the painful details of your dissertation. They get it, they'll probably even treat you to a beer. What they really want to know is the "now what"? What will you do with this line of inquiry? Where are you going from here?

If you are a finalist for a research-based appointment, you'll refer to your research statement or at least the information in your statement in many interview venues. Myriad groups will want to learn of your research interests, research projects, and future plans. You should have no hesitation on your part to articulate your passion and knowledge of your research.

> *"A well-crafted statement helps us see your passion and your depth of knowledge in a particular interest area. We only want to hire people who will become productive scholars. In order to be productive, you need to have a handle on what you will be doing in the first three years as a junior professor."*
> *~Chair, Search Committee*

So how long should a research statement be? It's good idea to ask your faculty for advice on this. We know that there are some highly effective research statements that barely scratch the bottom of one page, while others in the STEM fields (Science, Technology, Engineering and Math) can be a minimum of ten pages. You don't want to look like you don't understand or know the field. Hopefully, your adviser will have a few samples from your discipline that you might review. Be sure to ask what they think is good about them and what they believe the shortcomings to be.

Research & Teaching Agendas

One job advertisement asks for a Research Agenda; the other one requires a Research Plan; yet another calls for my Teaching Agenda. How many statements do I need to prepare? How different are they? As a job seeker, you are basically preparing a *map* or a *chart* that outlines what you are doing in your niche and what you anticipate doing in the future. These documents are the perfect vehicle to state your research and goals, to outline the approach you intend to take, and to confirm its importance in the "bigger picture" in your discipline.

> *"No hype, no exaggerations. Someone on the hiring committee will be knowledgeable in your field. Your documents must be able to withstand scrutiny from tenured professors who have spent the better part of their life examining similar topics."*
> *~Department Chair, Chemistry*

Some hiring committees will require a research agenda as well as a teaching agenda; others will specify one or the other. Why do hiring committees want all of these documents to review? Isn't this overload? The answer is simple. It is the business of hiring committees to locate candidates who have the ability to obtain tenure at their institution. As committee members review applications, these questions are always present: can this candidate succeed at our institution? Can this candidate offer the courses we need? Can this candidate conduct research? Get funding? Publish? Can this candidate participate in interdisciplinary projects? These questions are prevalent not only for the science-types, but also for the humanities scholars.

Many institutions will request a teaching agenda in addition to a philosophy statement. What is that? It is not, as some job seekers interpret, a lesson plan or sample agenda for a course. A teaching agenda is most often a description of short and long-terms goals with respect to your vision for teaching in a given discipline. This can include statements about courses you'd like to teach or feel particularly qualified to teach, courses you'd like to develop and teach in the future, opportunities for interdisciplinary coursework or offerings, and how you hope your vision for teaching and learning (here on the macro-level) will inform or serve the departmental goals. That's no small feat, we know. It requires not only that you delve into your own personal philosophy statement about teaching, (which you just did, remember) but it also requires that you apply that to a department that you probably don't know very well, composed of faculty who may have a different style than you do.

A teaching agenda is not a critique of the department to which you're applying, nor is it intended to give you full license to share your vision for the department, but rather meld your vision for teaching and learning and your knowledge of the discipline (including future directions) with their already stellar and solid programs. Sounds cheeky? Yep, but that's your job as a job seeker. They are the ones offering a job and deciding if you're a good fit. If your agenda comes off in an imperialistic or critical way, you may be hearing crickets.

Always consider your audience: You want to look like one of them. Your various documents provide of glimpse of who you are as a scholar and what you can contribute to their department and institution.

Think back to all the talks and colloquia you have attended over the past few years. No doubt some of these sessions helped you to generate new ideas or helped you to think about something in a fresh or different way. Your statements may have the same effect on your audiences.

There are a variety of formats that can be employed. Talk to your advisor to determine what is customary in your field. Your advisor has undoubtedly served on search committees and will be your best resource for learning about the expectations and issues that are particular to your field. There is variation in format and length from one discipline to another.

Tips for packaging agendas, plans and philosophies:

1. Use the same font as you used on your CV and letters.
2. Layout essentials include one inch margins, one font, and the use of headers/footers.
3. Make it interesting to read.
4. If graphics are used, label or caption graphics to assist the reader.
5. Clear, succinct—absolutely no possibility for reader to be confused.
6. Realistic. Is this plan doable or is it hyperbole?
7. No mistakes or misrepresentations.
8. Proofread. Over and over.

Don't forget that these materials are just a few pages of probably thousands that your search committee will read before determining whom to bring to campus. Don't frustrate your search committee by forcing them to read poorly formatted, messy, or irrelevant information.

Interview Portfolios

Give your job search a little juice. A job search that utilizes the power of the web and an ePortfolio is like a job search on steroids. ePortfolios or other web-based resources that allow you to demonstrate your professional identity, when done right, can be the ticket that seals the deal for employers. Candidates who engage in the process of creating an ePortfolio are better able to relate their experience to an employer. The process of putting the portfolio together and reviewing prior to a campus visit or conference interview, helps you more easily recall the valuable experiences in academe that have made you who you are. We've been in your shoes. We know what your brain capacity is about now. Most of you are running on fumes (hopefully the legal kind). An ePortfolio allows you to succinctly communicate your potential by rising above simple annotations on a CV. Why not show your research paper or literature review from your advanced seminar class, or better yet, how about a video of some of your best teaching? An ePortfolio elevates a candidate to the next level because it reflects a process that communicates expertise in their field. Candidates are able to present a richer picture of themselves and search committees are better able to make employment decisions. The ease of use for the candidate, for the faculty member, and for the search committee is unparalleled. An ePortfolio is undeniably essential.

An online portfolio combines the integration of technologies, scholarship, teaching, and service. Your ePortfolio provides the architecture within which you can demonstrate competence in your academic discipline and showcase your strengths to a range of relevant audiences including search committees and hiring officials at national and international levels. The framework allows you the opportunity to provide authentic evidence of scholarly work and to highlight academic strengths and achievement by linking artifacts to your ePortfolio by using web and multimedia technologies.

> *"A candidate with an online portfolio can enter an academic career with a set of integrated digital tools that afford short-term career advantages and long-term professional benefits."*
> *~Department Chair, English Education*

Portfolio Artifacts

ePortfolios allow you to provide more information to search committees in a way that's super convenient. Imagine that long list of articles linked to the publications themselves. Or, what if your presentation titles fascinate me, but I want to know more than just the titles – BINGO – link them to a pdf version or podcast of your presentation. Your ePortfolio adds richness both in terms of content and media variety that is unavailable in your CV. Bring your CV to life! It's like FrankenCV.

Your ePortfolio allows you to have your file cabinet or your hard-drive at your fingertips. What an advantage!

As you organize your ePortfolio for the academic job search remember your audience and strive to organize it in a way that makes sense to search committees. Most institutions are interested primarily in the following areas:

Credentials
- Degrees
- Licenses
- Certificates
- Scholarships
- Distinctions
- Employment
- Practica
- Internships
- Externships
- Fellowships

Teaching
- Philosophy
- Agenda
- Experiences
- Teaching Assistantships
- Syllabi
- Video Demonstrations
- Evaluations

Research
- Statement
- Agenda/Plan
- Dissertation
- Experiences
- Research Assistantships
- Lab Protocols
- Posters
- Presentations
- Papers
- Publications

Service
- Philosophy
- Leadership
- Academic Service
- Community Outreach
- Professional Service

What if this hierarchy became the backbone of your portfolio design? Individuals can create effective ePortfolios using web-based hosting services, like Interfolio, that specialize in web-based portfolios for the academic professional community. Some also choose to create such tools using Google's wide assortment of web-based and free tools, blogs, or pay web-hosting services. Most of these options do the html design for you. The hard part for you is determining an effective structure (hint hint, use the one we just talked about) and then finding relevant and meaningful and, most importantly, marketable artifacts that will sell you as the next Doctor of the Universe! Take a look at this abbreviated list of artifacts:

- *Publications*
- *Presentations*
- *Performances*
- *Syllabi*
- *Student Evaluations*
- *Experimental Protocols*
- *Summary Tables*
- *Teaching Philosophy*
- *Academic Papers*
- *Assessment Instruments*
- *Collaborative Projects*
- *Experiment Designs*
- *Field Notes*
- *Laboratory Projects*
- *Media Integration*
- *Summative Appraisals*
- *Reflective Statements*
- *Products of Presentations (papers, summaries, outlines, abstracts)*
- *Writing Abstracts*
- *Summarized Research*
- *Employment Listing*
- *Internships*
- *Externships*
- *Fellowships*
- *Products of Student Learning*
- *Social Media Links*
- *Expanded Research Agenda*
- *Abstracts*
- *Presentation Slides*
- *Teaching Videos*
- *Lectures on iTunes*
- *Graphs*
- *Charts*
- *Bibliographies*
- *Case Studies*
- *Clinical Reports*
- *Evaluation Data*
- *Evaluation Instruments*
- *Interdisciplinary Research*
- *Language Proficiencies & Evidence*
- *Tutorial/Laboratory Activities*
- *Student Performance Data*
- *Lab/Technical Reports*
- *Teaching Materials (syllabi, rubrics, grading policies, media resources, online sources)*
- *Art Products (exhibits, juried shows, invitational exhibitions, group shows)*
- *Artwork Slides*
- *Images of Art/Performance*
- *Conducting Video*
- *Grant Abstracts*
- *External Funding Reports*
- *Leadership Experiences*

Again, we could go on and on about the kinds of artifacts that you could use as evidence that you're the next best Jr. faculty member. The bottom line is that your artifacts have to serve the purpose. If they're supposed to get you a job – don't use your worst paper from your least favorite professor. Use artifacts and examples of your work that you are excited about, that you feel tell your story, and that communicate your passion.

Inappropriate ePortfolio Materials

Understand that for a search committee, you are what's in your ePortfolio. If your ePortfolio doesn't do the job of showcasing your experiences in a positive and affirming light, don't use it. Keep it for your own records. Irrelevant artifacts or an unnecessarily narcissistic focus on your personal life, including hobbies (or hubbies) tends to be a waste of valuable search-committee time. Don't get us wrong; people love finding out all the weird personal things we do in our lives, and most search committee members would probably admit to doing a little cyber-stalking, but it's not wise to give them ammo or strangely irrelevant information.

We live in an age where much of the distinction between personal and professional appears to be cloudy, but it absolutely is not. Employment laws, human resource offices, and even your future students' parents are prepared to address a whole array of infractions on this personal-professional divide. Focus your ePortfolio artifacts on relevant and professional examples of your work. Avoid the following on your ePortfolio:

- *Digital images of you or others in non-relevant situations*
- *References to your citizenship, nationality, race, ethnicity, language, height, weight, sexuality, gender identity, and political affiliation.*
- *Personally identifying numbers (like you might find on your driver's license, visa)*
- *Tasteless or insensitive material (not everyone thinks that's funny)*
- *Information that's a violation of FERPA: student records, grades, images or videos of students without their permission*
- *Links to personal social media that may compromise your search*
- *Copyrighted material that's not appropriately attributed*
- *Page animations that are distracting (snowfall, background songs)*
- *Religious or political references*
- *An app or widget that tells you where visitors are from*
- *Scanned or digital copies of transcripts, licenses, or other certificates (this can lead to professional identity theft)*
- *Letters of recommendation or references*
  (Folks usually do not want their contact information broadcast over the internet and posting your letters of recommendation from faculty could be the kiss of death for your job search.)
- *Irrelevant undergraduate artifacts, or even worse, links to your high school experiences.*

Social Media and your ePortfolio

Raise your hand if you have a Facebook page. Exactly! Most of you are probably raising your hand (we hope you're in a public place like a coffee shop). Keep your hand up if you are connected to at least one person who is also within your professional circle. Chances are, most of you still have a hand in the air (hopefully you didn't forget your deo today). Now, raise your other hand if you have liked a professional association page, have multiple professional 'friends', or use Facebook in coursework, or other sorts of professional activities. Chances are most of you now have both hands in the air. Ok, do the Hokey Pokey, 'cause that's what it's all about (these days).

Social media is transforming the way we connect, share, and take in information. Most who use these tools on a frequent basis would indicate that they feel more informed, or plugged into their professional world because of this media. Most of these platforms, however, do not lend themselves to helping you organize a valuable job-seeking and interview portfolio. Facebook isn't organized around the categories of Teaching, Research and Service. Nope. For this reason, we recommend using another tool that gives you more control over how you format your work. These social sites also are not into hosting your artifacts, be they pdfs, video demonstrations, or the like. You'd have to find a separate hosting service for those documents anyway.

Facebook, Twitter, LinkedIn, and the multitude of other social media represent ways that you can begin to establish connections with folks in your profession either directly, by friending them, or indirectly, by liking their unit, department, organization and other similar sorts of pages. Once you become a member or like these pages, consider adding relevant and meaningful and dare we say 'fun' comments. But beware: what you consider funny, another may consider completely insulting. Keep your comments brief and to the point. Academics appreciate brevity, especially when reading someone else's words.

Develop a site, share it with social media.

Use your hosting service to create a powerful professional image, and then use the power of social media to get that image out there. Blogs and other professional forums also provide you an opportunity to share your professional opinion in ways that can help get you noticed: make sure that you have a professional presence that makes linking from one site to another seamless for a person cyber-stalking you. In other words, if you choose to comment on various blogs, make sure you also create a blog account so that folks can click on your user name. Once they get to your blog, you provide links and access to other professional, or internet depots where you share a bit more information. Your internet identity is a bit like a system of airline hubs. The most successful airlines have multiple hubs, easy systems for check-in, and a manageable network of interrelated and interconnected spokes. However, several large airlines have gone bankrupt because their systems got way too big and unmanageable. Keep your online presence tight and well-groomed.

Getting your ePortfolio noticed:

- *List your URL on your CV: make it obvious and stand out.*
- *Develop your Facebook page and manage your privacy settings such that anything folks shouldn't see isn't visible.*
- *Use your Facebook and other social media to establish a visibly connected image (when I open your Facebook or LinkedIn and notice lots of professional organizations, I might think: This person is connected! I might also think, this person wastes a lot of time). Balance is key.*
- *Avoid creating so many clicks to get to your ePortfolio that I get lost or lose interest along the way. One should easily click from social media to your ePortfolio only once.*
- *Once I get to your ePortfolio, make sure you provide me a way out by linking back to your social media.*
- *Include mention of your ePortfolio in a cover letter.*
- *Share your ePortfolio with key faculty members. Seek their advice and ask them to share your URL with peers.*
- *Include your URL on a business card. If you don't have a business card yet, make one and take advantage of every opportunity to distribute your business card at professional meetings, seminars and conferences.*
- *Actively incorporate your ePortfolio into your job-search preparation. Use it to prepare for interviews, analyze your work, and think about your professional goals! That way when asked, you'll have something definitive to say.*
- *Use social media to connect to others in your field and utilize department websites to maximize your potential to get them away from outdated newsletters to your up-to-date online self.*

Notes

Notes

Interviews, Offers & Negotiations

PhD Planner

PART 3: INTERVIEWS, OFFERS & NEGOTIATIONS

Part 3 of *The PhD Handbook for the Academic Job Search* focuses on preparing you for the screening, selection, and hiring process. It's not always absolutely clear in the academy how search committees make their choices. But we have some winning strategies to help you make the most of the various interview scenarios in which you'll strive to shine. In this section you'll learn about: the art of interviewing in various settings, doing your homework, the most common interview questions, job talks and the on-campus visit, dining situations, and how to interpret offers and carefully negotiate with your future colleagues.

18	**Employer Profile** Advanced interview homework
19	**On-Campus Visit** Advanced interview preparation
20	**Interview Notes** The basic questions you have to nail
21	**Apparel and Packing Planner** Looking good was never this easy
22	**Community Inventory** Can I live here?
23	**Academic Negotiations** There's more to this than salary Part 1
24	**Academic Negotiations** There's more to this than salary Part 2
25	**My Thank You List** A little thanks goes a long way

Note: PhD Planner numbers **12 — 17** that were discussed in part two of this handbook make excellent interview rehearsal and preparation guide sheets. We know you're too busy to do those again, so look back on those planner pages as you prepare for interviews.

Interviews: The Art of Selling You

Cue music from the classic movie "2001: A Space Odyssey." You know the one with the exaggerated timpani drum that follows a dramatic trumpet building into a full orchestral crescendo. Those of you in music will recognize the true title to the piece, think Strauss' *Also Sprach Zarathustra*. As you approach the team of interviewers, you think to yourself: *I'm about to land on the moon.* You envision yourself wearing an indestructible space suit. You are about to make history. You are about to take one large step toward launching your career.

There is some justification for placing so much importance on the personal interview. All of the preceding stages aim toward this encounter. No CV, cover letter, or dossier will get you a job; their purpose is to stimulate an employer's interest in your qualifications so that a face-to-face meeting will be arranged. Now it's your turn to seal the deal, but this process is fraught with all sorts of "craters." Critical as each stage of the selection process may be, most job seekers express particular anxiety about the interview. We could spend time sharing with you some ideas for *stress-busting*, but at this stage in the game, hopefully, you've figured out what works for you and what doesn't. You've been at this for a while now, and getting the job is only the beginning. Remember that analogy we made earlier in the book about the job search being a little bit like dating? Well, come on, have fun with it. If you don't act like you're having fun and doing what you love, you'll never convince a search committee to hire you.

How do you react and respond to stress? The success of your interview may depend largely on how you manage stress in these sorts of situations.

Whether you are a first-time job seeker or an experienced professional, you probably do not consider yourself an expert on the subject of interviewing. It is important to recognize that some of the people responsible for hiring do not have a great deal of experience in conducting interviews, either. In many cases, especially in the academic world, they are teachers, researchers, practitioners, or administrators, not human resources specialists. Mostly, it's important to remember, that if you've been offered an interview of either variety (screening or selection), it's a huge compliment to your talent and potential. Don't blow it.

Doing Your Homework

It never fails. Candidates show up for an on-campus interview looking like they just stepped out of a GQ ad. They seem to have done everything right. And then they open their mouth. At first the search committee thinks: *jet lag, stress.* Maybe they had a drink to calm their nerves on the plane. And then the candidate talks some more. The search committee tries to make excuses in their minds because they know the wad the department has just spent to bring *their favorite candidate* to campus. And then the candidate talks some more and you get a little pissed, because it's apparent that they have absolutely not done any homework, nor do they really seem to be that interested in what you do here. The committee feels a little betrayed.

A basic step toward successful interviewing is learning as much as you can about the institution or organization and the specific department in which the vacancy exists. Gathering information from the institution's website can benefit you in several ways as you prepare for the interview. When you do your homework in advance of an interview you: get a better sense of who they are, so that you can do a better job of convincing them why they want you and how you'll fit in. Remember, you want this job offer even if you don't want to take the job. The job offer puts the power in your hands, or the ball in your court (maybe for the first time since you started graduate school).

"Given the wealth of information available about colleges/universities via the Internet, there's no excuse for going into an interview underprepared. Spend the requisite time learning about the academic unit in which you'll be interviewing. Your knowledge and preparation will impress the search committee and better qualify you to determine whether you want to work here."

~Department Chair, Educational Leadership and High Education

Once you have identified faculty members or other personnel in the department you hope to join, you can do a thorough review of their track record, including, publications (do you know any of the co-authors?), books, leadership positions, teaching responsibilities, mentoring and advising experience, and so on and so forth. Don't stop there! Hopefully, you'll be able to quickly link to some of the published articles of the folks you'll meet. You don't need to go back three decades, unless their work was seminal and life changing for the rest of us, but taking a quick peek at what the last five or so years have produced for your faculty hosts (especially the ones you'll be spending a lot of time with) is a good investment of your time. No one has ever been too knowledgeable for an interview, but many job seekers have found reasons to regret their inadequate preparation.

Your homework assignment doesn't stop with your lit review of the faculty in the department. Take a look at the institutional profile of faculty members across the university or college. How many new or assistant faculty members do you see in other departments? Do they seem to be engaged in interdisciplinary work? Once you get your on-campus interview schedule, research every single line. You've been training for several years now on how to read between the lines. Apply this analytical and deductive reasoning skill to your campus interview preparation.

Students play an important role in your career (duh, right). Frankly, though, we are amazed at how many candidates can make it several hours into an interview before mentioning, discussing, or even referring to students. The interview is an inherently self-important process, we get it. But don't go even ten minutes into an interview without mentioning your excitement to meet with students (be they undergraduate, graduate, or both). They are the reason academe exists. Search department websites for student profiles, club affiliations, and evidence that students are the life-blood of the department. Review institutional data on admissions, enrollment trends, and retention/graduation rates. Does your department seem to offer scholarships, research opportunities, immersion learning experiences, and other sorts of high level engagement activity for students? If so, there's a good chance they heart students. What's the typical plan of study for undergraduate or graduate students? Where do you see your expertise fitting into the "student" plan? How can you teach majors, minors, and students in general education courses this department offers?

Don't even get ten minutes into an interview without mentioning or asking about the students you'll hopefully soon be teaching.

A good interview doesn't just happen. In order to make the situation work for you, it is essential that you devote some time to planning and preparing for each of the elements involved in the interview process. Because every interview will be different, you will need to prepare for each one individually; however, in spite of the differences, all interviews share common features, including discussions of the campus you're visiting, so know something about it.

A good interview doesn't just happen. The more you know, the better you will be in a competitive interview environment.

Gathering data prior to an interview just makes sense. Dig deep in the institution's website and college and local newspapers and you'll find the answers to most of the items listed below:

Job Interview Research Topics			
☐	Enrollment & Student Success	☐	Key Faculty & Administration
☐	Aid Allotment	☐	Placement Rates & Career Opportunities
☐	Diversity of Faculty and Students	☐	Accreditation
☐	Strengths of the Department	☐	Endowments & Donor Relations
☐	Student Population	☐	Strategic Plan & Vision
☐	Institutional Funding	☐	Institutional Type

As you can see from the exhaustive list above, you have quite a bit of work cut out for you. This is all probably in addition to dissertation writing, teaching or research assistantships and the like. Spending serious time getting to know as much as you can about the community you're about to visit has a calming effect. You'll arrive more prepared and ready to answer the questions right, and ready to ask the right questions.

The Interview

The only compliment greater than getting an interview, is getting the job offer. You should take the offer to interview as a significant validation of your time, effort, and investment in your doctoral program. There are several kinds of interviews: from the on-campus visit, to the phone interview, to the web-based Skype interviews, to our favorite, the airport interview. Each interview setting has its own idiosyncrasies and needs to which one should pay special attention. The key to success, regardless of the setting, mode, or amount of time is to know yourself, and to make a connection with the search team.

Interviews can be sorted into two general categories: screening interviews with the intention of whittling the pool down to a relatively manageable number of candidates; the second general category is the selection interview. In this type of interview, the goal is to determine if the candidate before the committee is *the* candidate for the job, department, and students. Screening and selection interviews generally occur in different kinds of settings, have different budgetary costs, and are often seen as different tasks by the interviewers. One is designed to cut, the other to select. The stakes are simply different for all involved.

Screening Interviews

Whether conducted at professional conferences or on college campuses, screening interviews are usually brief, some no more than 20 minutes in length. Both the interviewer and the applicant should be prepared to channel their energies toward an exchange of information which will most efficiently use the allotted time. In-depth interviewing is not the goal; minor details will probably not be discussed and there may not be time for comments or questions about the college, community, or geographic area. Screening interviews, to be productive, must be limited in scope and are designed to probe a few key qualifications that have been gleaned from your CV or other application materials. You have 30 minutes to make a new best friend, or group of friends. This interview is all about personality. Can you make friends in 30 minutes?

Conference interviews are common in many professions because they are economically advantageous to the employer as well as to the applicant: you're going to be there already, along with a bazillion other eager beaver candidates. It's like a clearance sale at Target. Most conference interviews are prearranged, though some occur as a result of a placement activity through the professional association (everyone has to make money these days). Depending on the conference, you'll either be meeting in a hotel room or a reserved meeting room (generally on-site). At first, it seems a little weird walking into a hotel room for an interview, but after-all, we are all a little weird here, right? You should dress as you would for any serious face-to-face interview. We recommend professional suiting for the interview itself. If you are interviewing at a conference, consider every waking minute at the conference a part of the interview. This will sound psycho, sorry, but someone is always watching you. Sorry folks, save the sweats for the gym and the yoga pants for yoga class.

If you are a graduate student, you should be sure faculty members from your department know that you are attending the conference and that you are available for interviews. Their contacts with colleagues from other institutions can be extremely helpful in arranging interviews. You should also share news of a conference interview with them immediately. Let them know how to reach you during the conference. Your primary purpose in attending the conference may be to interview for as many jobs as possible, but you should also plan to attend meetings and sessions related to your interests and areas of specialization. It's time to network and shake hands with as many folks as you can, even when it feels like torture to walk past the Starbucks and those sticky buns. There is always the chance that participation in informal discussions can lead to a job prospect, sticky buns will not. Be visible, be assertive, and be professional, and don't hesitate to let people know you are looking for a job.

Skype, Web-Conference & Phone Interviews

A new trend in hiring has shifted some of the screening interviews to web-based services like Skype or other web-conferencing software (polycom, adobe connect, etc.). These are inexpensive techniques that allow committees to discover invaluable information about a select group of candidates. Since many faculty searches will elicit hundreds of applications, certainly not every candidate will have their chance to meet with a search committee over Skype, but it's not unreasonable for committees to screen down to five to ten candidates for web-based or phone interviews. These interviews have two clearly defined purposes: to get a sense of an individual's interpersonal style, and to screen out those who don't fit the bill. It's complicated to judge an individual's interpersonal style over the phone. Search committees are listening for articulate answers, a warm and inviting style, enthusiasm for the interview and institution, and honesty and integrity in your interview answers. We make the joke in a live seminar we give, that in face-to-face settings, candidates need to smile with their eyes while interviewing. Over the phone, candidates need to smile with their voices.

QUICK TIPS

YES

- If you offer a Skype interview or agree to one, you better learn it. Like Now.
- Make sure your phone message is appropriate.
- Create a space that is free of distractions, interruptions, and the potential to seem unprofessional (do not interview in your bed).
- Be someplace that offers the greatest phone reception or bandwidth.
- Turn off any pop-ups on your computer or phone. That's distracting and disrespectful.
- Have your entire dossier (CV, job ad, cover letter, teaching philosophy, research agenda, etc.) at your fingertips. Extra pad and paper too. Take notes, even if it's a short interview.
- Be prepared to ask questions and make lots of eye contact with the camera.
- Log on well in advance to make sure all systems are go: sound, camera, etc.

NO

- Don't let your eyes wander. It looks weird on your web-camera when we see lots of eye-white (did you just roll your eyes?)
- Do a quick *set check* before your web-cam interview. Maybe that window behind you is a bad idea (are you trying to look dramatic with the backlighting?) Those cheap curtains are distracting a member of the search team.
- Even though you may be interviewing in your living room, don't appear as if you just rolled out of bed. Take web and phone interviews just as seriously with regard to dress as you would as if you were in person.
- Tidy up your surroundings if at home and if in your office, kindly let your fellow office-mates know that they aren't allowed in the office that morning (explain why of course).

Phone and web-based interviews present a whole new level of complication. The technology and interface may pose a credible barrier to individuals who aren't completely conversant in how a certain program works. Bottom line: know the technology, especially if you offer.

Most candidates report that it's easier to focus when you're only talking to one person on the other end of the line. Conference-style phone interviews can be kind of tricky when multiple people try to speak at the same time (and given who you're talking to, they will all want to speak simultaneously). It's imperative to use the best quality phone line (connection) as possible. If it's easier for you to concentrate and look through your CV or dossier while you speak to folks on the phone, make sure your speakerphone settings are adjusted to optimal settings and that your paper shuffling isn't causing more unnecessary and distracting background noise. This is one reason why advance planning and preparation, like anticipating interview questions and rehearsing them, is so important. When you are speaking to a whole room full of people using internet video, be sure to make eye contact with each of them, even though it may be hard to know who exactly is talking, and at whom exactly, you should be looking. Use your pad and paper to scribble down the names of the individuals so that you can refer to them by name (specifically when it's time for you to ask some questions). It's impressive to learn names so quickly. If your phone, conference, or web-based screening interview was a success, you'll be invited for an on-campus visit. Before we get into the details of that experience, here's your homework list:

Before the Interview	
GOALS:	• Get the on-campus visit. • Make a connection with all involved in the screening process be it over phone, web, or in person. • Smile.
HOMEWORK:	• Know everyone you'll be talking to. • Anticipate their questions (know your dissertation, research, teaching, and professional goals). • Do some sort of stress-buster activity prior to your screening interview. • Discuss your screening interview with your advisor: they may have special insight and encouragement never hurts.

Selection Interviews: The On-campus Visit

After the pool of applicants for a given position has been screened through preliminary interviews or evaluation of each candidate's dossier, the finalists will be invited for a comprehensive, detailed interview or series of interviews on the college campus. For academic positions, it is not uncommon for an interview to extend to two full days or even longer. If you are invited for an on-site or campus interview at the employer's location, you can expect that the field has been narrowed to a select group of candidates, although the exact number of finalists will vary with the nature of the organization and the level of the position.

> *"Once you have made it to an on-campus interview, you have a good chance of getting an offer. Rarely do we bring more than four candidates on campus for the selection interview. Prepare. Be ready. Be sharp and make a connection."*
> ~Professor of English, Chair Faculty Search

During the course of a selection interview, you can expect to meet with several different individuals from across the department and campus. Search committees are generally comprised of administrators, faculty members from one or more departments, and professional staff members. Occasionally, other members of the committee may include staff, students, or other interested parties who serve in a non-voting or ex-officio capacity. Regardless of the size or makeup of the search committee, all committees will have a designated head, sometimes called the chair, under whose direction responsibilities are divided among the voting members, generally an odd number. Typical responsibilities of a search committee include:

- Creating and disseminating the job description
- Reviewing applications (typically online)
- Selecting individuals to be interviewed
- Conducting interviews
- Post-interview evaluation and ranking of candidates
- Affirmative action review
- Recommendation of final candidates
  (ranked list or a selected individual)

On-campus Visit Goals Worksheet	
GOALS:	• Arrive on campus, rested and prepared to be an effective interviewee. • Make eye contact, smile, and communicate your enthusiasm for being invited to campus and meeting these potential colleagues. • Determine how personal and professional inventories match the host. • Be a gracious guest: acknowledge all who are present at a talk or social event and be sure to thank your hosts for their hospitality and interest.
HOMEWORK:	• Learn who the decision-makers will be. • Ask follow-up questions about the department, expectations of you, tenure process (support and promotion), teaching and research. • Know the timeline for the search committee to reach a decision.

In most cases, search committees do not have the power to hire. It is their function to recommend one or more candidates to the administrator, usually the dean or provost, who is ultimately responsible for hiring, subject to approval by the governing board of the institution or organization.

Budgeting your On-Campus Visit

Have you ever gone to the grocery store, filled up your cart, and then as you approach the check-out counter you realize you forgot your purse or wallet? This has happened to lots of us…perhaps our hunger for food sometimes trumps our ability to plan effectively for such events. Likewise, your hunger for a job might cloud your ability to approach your search, especially once you've reached the hot seat on-campus visit. Colleges and universities handle costs and expenses associated with the on-campus visit in different ways. Some colleges will request that you make your own arrangements to be reimbursed following your visit. Always have enough cash on hand to cover both expected and unexpected expenses. Travel and lodging represent the major portion of interview expenses but meals, cabs, and other incidentals can add up to a considerable sum.

Make sure money isn't an issue during your campus visit by planning ahead and being independent.

Keep all of your receipts for tax purposes or to be returned with your travel vouchers if you are to be reimbursed. Some institutions will reimburse you for any related interviewing expenses; others specify exactly what will be covered. There may be restrictions on reimbursement. For example, if the job is offered and you accept the offer, all expenses may be paid. If you decline the offer, the institution may reimburse you for half of the cost, or none at all. Talk about a strong message: *Don't waste our time coming here to interview if you are not interested.* Before you accept an invitation to interview, make sure you understand the financial arrangements.

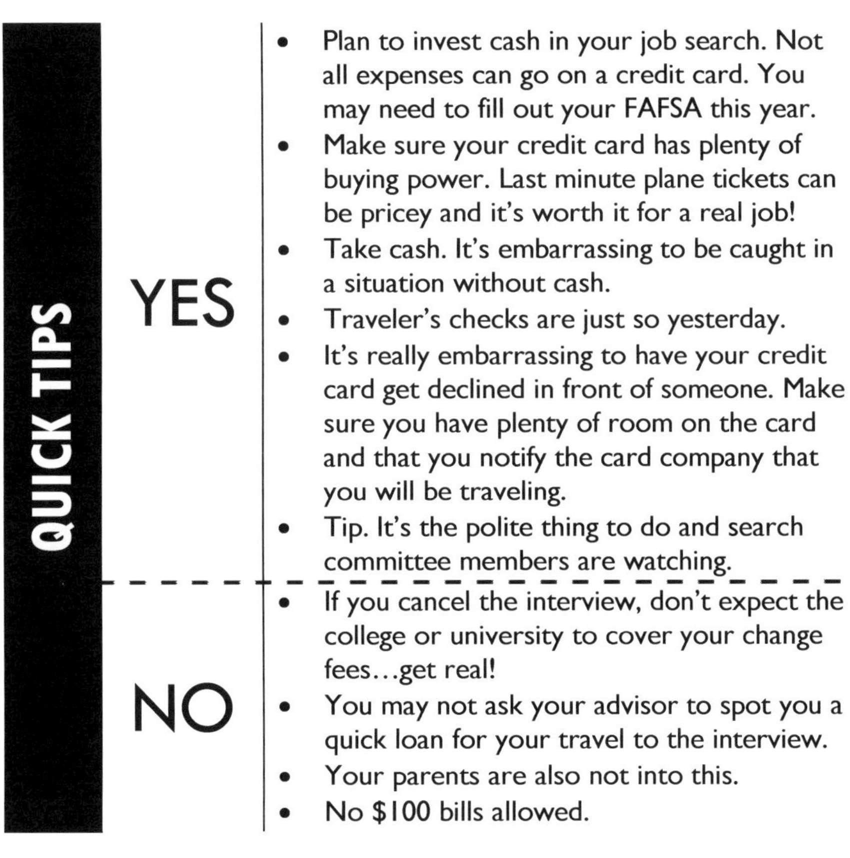

QUICK TIPS

YES

- Plan to invest cash in your job search. Not all expenses can go on a credit card. You may need to fill out your FAFSA this year.
- Make sure your credit card has plenty of buying power. Last minute plane tickets can be pricey and it's worth it for a real job!
- Take cash. It's embarrassing to be caught in a situation without cash.
- Traveler's checks are just so yesterday.
- It's really embarrassing to have your credit card get declined in front of someone. Make sure you have plenty of room on the card and that you notify the card company that you will be traveling.
- Tip. It's the polite thing to do and search committee members are watching.

NO

- If you cancel the interview, don't expect the college or university to cover your change fees…get real!
- You may not ask your advisor to spot you a quick loan for your travel to the interview.
- Your parents are also not into this.
- No $100 bills allowed.

Knowing your Interview Itinerary

When you accept an invitation to interview, it is important to be aware of the interview schedule or timetable. Getting your on-campus visit itinerary means it's *game-on* for your visit preparation. The invitation may be accompanied by a detailed schedule of events, but if the information is incomplete or sketchy, asking the following questions is not only appropriate but essential for interview success.

- May I have the names of the search committee members?
- What functions will be arranged? Job Talk? Teaching Demo?
- Will I have the opportunity to meet with graduate or undergraduate students?
- What special functions will be arranged (reception, dinner, one-on-one with Dean, lunch with graduate students)?

Of course, make sure you review the schedule before proceeding to ask any of these questions. If your schedule includes lunch with graduate students, you can assume that this will be the primary opportunity for you to meet with that population. Your preparation, the materials that you bring along, the wardrobe you select, and the arrangements for transportation and hotel accommodations hinge on basic schedule information. Social functions including receptions or meals may be arranged to allow the applicant to meet potential colleagues. It is important to realize that social functions are part of the selection process. Guests are evaluating your social adeptness, poise, and personality. Keep in mind that committee members are looking for approachable colleagues.

> *"Everyone knows that first impressions are important. Some candidates view the major events on an itinerary as important but don't recognize that each event on an itinerary is an opportunity to make a good first impression."*
>
> ~Professor of American Studies, Chair Faculty Search

As you peruse the interview itinerary, you'll quickly see that you'll have very little free time. Finding a few minutes to visit the bathroom will be a luxury. In addition to having copies of your CV and your job-talk handouts in your portfolio/briefcase, stick in a couple of protein bars, some breath mints, and a small bottle of vitamin water. When you get that bathroom break, eat your protein bar. You'll be too busy concentrating and talking during lunch to eat much so you need to take advantage of every opportunity you have to keep your energy up. Candidates who try to subsist on Starbucks coffee all day end up getting dehydrated and displaying strange ticks. That's an interview no-no.

Sample On-Campus Interview Itinerary

Agenda for Will B. Fine
Position # 11264: Assistant Professor French

Wednesday, February 2, 201x	
4:00 pm	Dr. Olaf Anders; meet at airport arrivals "B"
5:00 pm	Tour of Campus City
7:30 pm	Dinner with Search Committee-Hotel Z

Thursday, February 3, 201x	
7:30 am	Graduate student picks up at hotel (TJ Stubbs)
8:00 am	Breakfast with Dean Bea Goode, City Center Café
9:30 am	Meeting with graduate student representatives
10:30 am	Interview with DEO Dr. Able Scholar
Noon	Lunch with invited faculty, staff & students
1:30 pm	Job Talk
3:00 pm	Free time
3:30 pm	Interview with Search Committee members
5:00 pm	Building tour-host graduate student (TJ Stubbs)
7:00 pm	Reception and dinner, Hotel Z, with selected faculty

Friday, February 4, 201x	
8:00 am	Breakfast meeting with school-based partners *(School Board Office, South Chicago Ave)*
9:30 am	Teaching Demonstration, 212 College Hall
11:00 am	Tour of campus with graduate student (TJ Stubbs)
12:00 pm	Luncheon Interview with Grants Director Elena Kazakhstan and Vice President So Ahn So
1:30 pm	Final interview with Dean Bea Goode
3:30 pm	Transportation to airport—Meet in lobby of Hotel Z (driver: Stu DeBaker, graduate student)
5:00 pm	Arrive at airport/Depart on flight AA 397

Hotel Information:
Hotel Z
123 Capital Street
Anytown, Anystate
Tel: 123.456.7891
Email: hotelz@hotelz.com
Hotel-Z.com

Flight Information:
American Fl. 396
Dep: 13:00
Arr: 15:45

American Fl. 397
Dep: 18:00
Arr: 20:00

Campus Contacts:
Dr. So Ahn So
Office: 123.223.2323
Cell: 123.233.3232

Dr. Wally Waldo
Office: 123.323.3232
Cell: 123.345.6767

By closely examining your itinerary, you can make each moment of your academic interview more productive by better engaging your audience, feeling more confident and capable because you are well-prepared, and focusing on what matters during your campus visit: building relationships. A closer look at the itinerary will reveal several key elements you should research:

> - Your flight arrival information (consider whether checking a bag is in your best interest, probably not).
> - Who's on the search committee? (don't worry about who will be at dinner: you should know all members of the search committee: research, responsibilities, role in department).
> - Does the department have a webpage devoted to graduate students? Who is this TJ Stubbs anyway? Try to cyberstalk their Facebook, but don't friend them yet.
> - What is the Dean like…does she tweet? Facebook? Is there information about her background? It might be nice to find something that you can connect over: you're both from Florida, you both work in the same area, or you both love Farmville (ok, that might be too stalkerish…).
> - Does the hotel have a hot tub (you may need it after a long day of interviewing…don't forget your swimsuit, but don't fall asleep in the pool and drown). That's a real downer for the search committee.
> - Who is Elena Kazakhstan? The Provost? You'll be meeting with them, you should probably try to learn about them.
> - Check out and print a campus map, in case TJ Stubbs ends up accidentally ditching you. It's good to have some key phone numbers, too. Make sure your phone is charged (and on silent).

Your itinerary will also reveal what sorts of formal presentations you should prepare in advance (your job talk and a teaching demonstration being the most common).

Job Talk & Presentations

When you are invited to an on-campus interview, you should be informed if a job talk or research presentation will be a part of your agenda (often these are one-in-the-same). Formal presentations may be made to the selection committee, to an audience of interested faculty, to graduate students, or to a mixed group of faculty and students. Whatever the audience, presentations will likely be one of two types: a teaching demonstration or a research presentation. Be sure to ask your interview contact who the audience for this particular presentation will be and make sure you know exactly how much time you have.

If you are asked to present your research, your dissertation is the place to start. Select a manageable topic from a section of your dissertation rather than attempting to present a thorough discussion of the entire project. Assume that your audience consists of both colleagues and students, and make the presentation accessible to scholars in other disciplines as well as to undergraduates. Reading a paper may be standard procedure at a professional conference; this presentation, however, usually needs a more interactive approach. People want to see your style.

> *Practice. Practice. Practice. Don't make naïve mistakes. The job talk is your exposure to an important group and they will make quick judgments about your abilities. Show your advisor your outline and get feedback. It's easy to get bogged down on the wrong thing for 20 minutes. You might shake and quiver as you are presenting—but if the content and preparation is coming through, you'll be ok. If you are not prepared, all the work you've done in graduate school can be wiped out in a matter of 20 minutes."*
>
> ~Professor of American Studies, Chair Faculty Search

More people screw up the job talk than any other part of the on-campus visit. Understand that most on-campus visits won't ask you to go into every fine detail of your research or research agenda. While you should be prepared to answer specific questions about your research, your preparation should focus on big picture, future projects, funding, and how your research fits into the institution. Job talk essentials include:

- Plan to use appropriate technology to present your research, but have a backup plan in the event of equipment or power failure. Keep your presentation simple, PowerPoint slides reasonable, and easy to read.
- Prepare a one-or two-page handout for the audience.
- Be prepared to answer questions about your choice of dissertation topic, research methodology, and the relevance of your conclusions.
- Plan to show how your research will inform your teaching and how your research relates to the department you seek to join.

While your methodology, statistical methods, or theoretical approach are absolutely key, you need to remember that your job talk is supposed to tell the whole story, from start to finish, while leaving some time for questions and discussion at the end. Take a look at the job-talk outline and time estimate that one doctoral candidate prepared for her campus visit.

Job Talk: 212 North Lunderberg Center, Audience: Open Invitation	
10:00	Settle time, distribute handouts, smile
10:02	Welcome provided by chair, Dr. Horebowitch, smile
10:05	Thank search committee, audience members, smile
10:06-10:15	Introduction to research, motivations, rationale for study, smile
10:15-10:25	Methodology, Limitations of Methodology/Study, smile
10:25-10:35	Data analysis, collection, results, smile
10:35-10:45	Conclusion, future, significant learning & development, smile
10:45-11:00	Questions/Discussion, smile

Many job seekers report that talking about their research during the on-campus interview is easier than talking about teaching. For most doc students, teaching came a bit later in their program, whereas, research has been there from day one. Remember those required research courses you started in year one? Remember the academic plan you put together with your advisor when you arrived on campus? You've been steeped in research for several years and chances are you can talk about your interests with some measure of confidence and even passion.

To be completely honest, we believe that PowerPoint presentations are often the kiss of death for job seekers. How many of you have been to a research presentation where seemingly meaningless and impossible to read data was projected on a screen? We are over it. Search committees are over it, and most importantly, your students are SO over it. Your presentation should be engaging, interesting, and should demonstrate good body language and lots of eye contact. You can convey a great deal over a handout that might be more readily accessible to your audience, anyway. Some worry about not showing a technological skill. Trust us, PowerPoint is not the skill you're wanting to sell. There are plenty of tools available to accentuate points you make during a presentation. Don't insult us with an overreliance on an old-school convention.

Teaching Demonstrations

You are about to enter the classroom for the first time. Are you wearing slick penny-loafers or tap shoes? What kind of teacher are you? Are you a classic academic, the sage on the stage, or are you a vaudeville act, an entertainer? An invitation to do a teaching demonstration should be interpreted as a huge opportunity to make a winning impression with students. Most search committees actively seek and value student input on candidates. We're seriously surprised at how many candidates don't take this aspect of the search serious enough and actively prepare and plan to meet with students. Give us an engaging, captivating and motivating presentation unless you've been specifically asked to "just lead a discussion." (Yawn).

> *"It's a tough gig! Be prepared. Practice. Students will be evaluating how you relate to them. You want to connect with the graduate students. After all, you might be working with them soon."*
> ~Chair and Professor of Biochemistry

Again, it's key to know your audience and whether it is composed of students, faculty, administrators, or a mixed group. Most of the time you'll want to strive to make the learning experience as authentic as possible: acknowledge that you're just meeting and getting to know the students, better yet, take a few minutes before you begin or during your opener to get to know the students (to start building relationships). Don't try to pretend you are best friends with the students, remember they just met you. As you move into the content that you're teaching, set the stage and provide any background information that the students may need. Hint: don't try to teach something that is out-of-control difficult, that could set you up for disaster. Usually, you'll be asked to teach something or provide a perspective that's already included in the course syllabus. Sometimes, you'll be invited to do something completely of your choosing. If you are allowed to choose, ask about which course you'll be presenting to and teach something that is connected. Remember: know your audience and ask questions; it shows a responsible interest in being a good teacher.

QUICK TIPS

YES

- Do ask the right questions: which course, how many students, where are they at in the content, should I teach what's on the syllabus or may I deviate?
- Include technology (but not PowerPoint): Have you used cell phones as clickers? YouTube? iPads in the classroom?
- If you plan to use technology, have a backup should it fail.
- Smile, engage the students, respond to them with affirmations. Build relationships!
- Thank them afterwards for being test dummies (but don't call them that). ☺

NO

- Even though you might be teaching a PhD seminar, don't plan to just discuss. Boring.
- Don't assign homework.
- Don't spend half the class talking about yourself. This happens more often than you think.
- Don't assume that the students will like you, or, if you are close in age, that you should relate to them as a peer. Be their future faculty, not friend.
- Don't bad-mouth or criticize the students after the class, "I'm surprised they didn't know …" That's a slap in the face to the faculty who normally teach that class.
- Don't be rigid. Remember they're just getting to know you. Don't forget to include HUMOR.

Don't forget about your philosophy statement that talked about your reasons for teaching and your ability to motivate and engage students. Your teaching demonstration should highlight your ability to work with students' varied backgrounds. While your short teaching demonstration may not be able to capture all you mentioned in your teaching philosophy (formal assessment, providing written or oral feedback, integrating course technologies, etc.), it should definitely reflect some elements of your philosophy. For example, how do you check for comprehension and use that feedback (formative assessment) to adapt instruction on the spot or reinforce complicated concepts? How do you facilitate peer-to-peer interaction? Practice your teaching demonstration and reflect on your teaching philosophy before you get to your interview.

Image: Clothing, Body Language & Presence

Do you shop at Gucci? The Gap? Goodwill? It doesn't matter where you shop, it's how you put the outfit together that counts, and in this market, folks are paying a lot of attention to the details. With hundreds of candidates to choose from, several of whom are invited to interview (selection or on-campus visit), the impression you make, the respect that you communicate with a top-notch interview suit, may score you points with search committee members. Academics aren't necessarily known for their wardrobe; in fact, many of the folks who will interview you may be in jeans, but don't forget: they already have the job, you don't.

Don't be misled by the habitual appearance of your faculty or academic colleagues. Because of the casual, more relaxed attitude about appearance that prevails on many campuses and the typical range of academic salaries, professors are rarely placed on anyone's best-dressed list. Those who do attempt to make a statement by the way they dress are likely to strive for an aura of nonconformity, shabby elegance, or genteel poverty.

When it comes to choosing interview attire don't cut corners.

Faculty are aware of the financial strain on graduate students and new professionals, but regardless of the employer's level of empathy, job seekers need to make a good first impression. Consciously or unconsciously, people do make judgments based on appearance and you need to look as good in person as you did on paper. Most job seekers assume that they will be spending money on the job search and interview expenses are accepted as a necessary budget item, but many job seekers are surprised to get the credit card statement in the mail with their new wardrobe purchases for the on-campus interview.

It's never inappropriate to slightly overdress. A suit, a nice briefcase/portfolio. Appropriate attire typically is a suit with simple and limited accessories. Male and female candidates are held to the same professional standard."

~Professor of Medicine, Chair Faculty Search

A suit, or at least a sports coat and tie, should be considered standard interview attire for men. For women, a suit is always appropriate: a suit with slacks or a skirt; a dress with a matching coat is like pressing the wardrobe easy button. Remember, tailoring a suit, hemming pants/slacks or any other small tailoring details can easily take up to two weeks. Plan ahead so you are not fussing about your outfits but rather concentrating on your job talk or your dissertation's last chapter. Most hotel rooms come with an ironing board and iron. Use them. If you don't know how to use them, find a YouTube video. Your campus visit will likely last at least a couple of days. You are not allowed to recycle shirts, blouses, ties, or socks. Think about ways in which you can change up a single suit. Maybe for your teaching demonstration, you take off your suit coat and roll up your sleeves. Be you. Be an individual. Be mindful that you are involved in a professional conversation where your goal is to get the job.

Bottom line: take the professional interview seriously and do your best to look top notch, professional, clean, and put together. Avoid looking high-maintenance: yes, some people take looking good to a whole new level, and in the end, look high maintenance. What does this mean? Well, for starters: avoid asking questions about your outfit, hair, food in teeth, etc. It's just a little too close for folks who've just met you.

"The academy celebrates individuality, but I'm amazed at the degree to which some candidates misunderstand the professional interview attire. We expect that you'll take your visit seriously: we're putting you in front of our president, provost, and other faculty."

~Professor of German, Chair Faculty Search

You should look put together, but if you have enough gel in your hair to reseal the Hoover Dam, you might be over-doing it (get it…hairdo…over 'do'ing it). Nevermind. Be 100% comfortable in your outfit, with your hair, your make-up, etc. We never recommend that candidates get a wardrobe or hair make-over the day before they leave campus. Practice interview answers in your suit if you're not used to wearing one. Practice tying a tie if you're not used to tying one. Shave and trim your beard, facial hair, leg hair, nose hair.

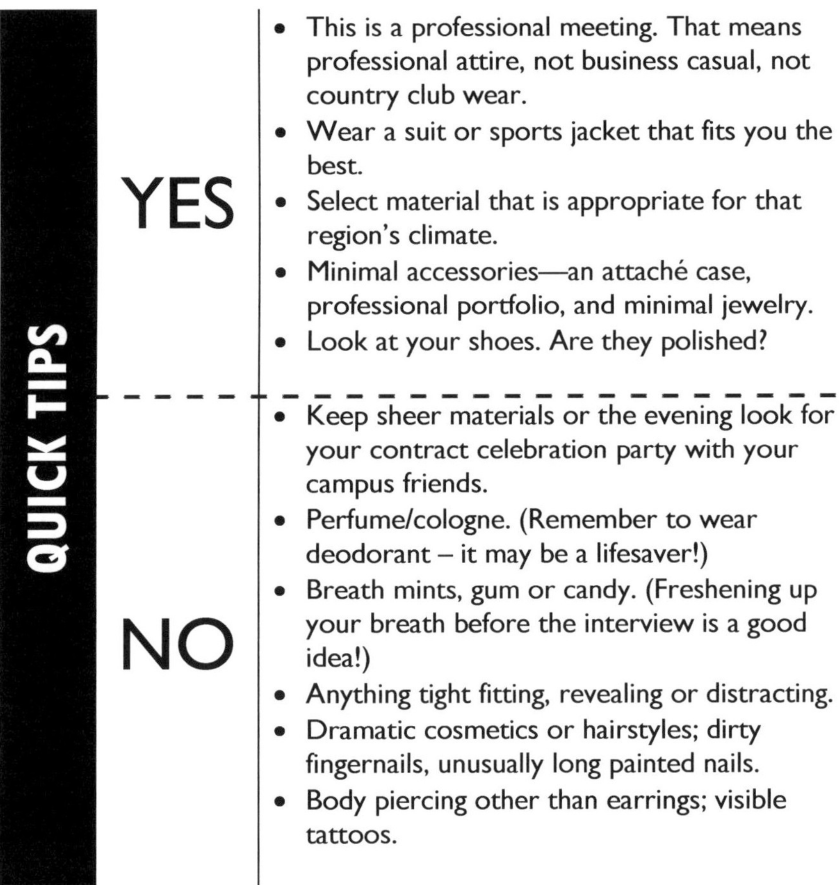

QUICK TIPS

YES	• This is a professional meeting. That means professional attire, not business casual, not country club wear. • Wear a suit or sports jacket that fits you the best. • Select material that is appropriate for that region's climate. • Minimal accessories—an attaché case, professional portfolio, and minimal jewelry. • Look at your shoes. Are they polished?
NO	• Keep sheer materials or the evening look for your contract celebration party with your campus friends. • Perfume/cologne. (Remember to wear deodorant – it may be a lifesaver!) • Breath mints, gum or candy. (Freshening up your breath before the interview is a good idea!) • Anything tight fitting, revealing or distracting. • Dramatic cosmetics or hairstyles; dirty fingernails, unusually long painted nails. • Body piercing other than earrings; visible tattoos.

Body Language

Do you realize how much you communicate non-verbally with your body? We know this to be true, yet so many job seekers are completely unaware of how much they communicate with their body. Look, we know that most of you are already mentally maxed out: dissertation, family stress, the prospect of a move, let alone getting ready for an on-campus interview. By the time you've purchased your suit, polished your shoes, found the perfect accessories, and prepared your talks, you are about ready to pass out. Thank god you have a long flight. Once you get to campus your mind is reeling with all sorts of other thoughts: *will they like me? How will I answer questions about my data? Will they buy my statistical methodology? Can I pretend to talk sports?* Suddenly, you have to think about how you're crossing your legs, too? Forget it. Well, unfortunately you can't forget about it because the entire campus visit is about your image, how people feel around you. Time to work your warm fuzzy maker.

Let's talk about the one area that so many brainy people have trouble with: eye contact. It all starts here. You have to make frequent eye contact with your audience whether it's one person or 10 people. We establish communication by meeting each other's gaze. If you have trouble looking others in the eye, you are going to appear insecure, aloof or even troubled. Some say that looking down or aside suggests evasion or a sense of insecurity. Looking up when asked a question, according to FBI profilers, suggests dishonesty. We know, academics who look up are thinking, but by the time you get to an interview, you should have thought about most of these questions already. Learn to smile with your eyes.

Smile with your eyes.

Use open gestures, avoid crossing your arms or putting your hands on your hips. Again, profilers say this demonstrates defiance. When you speak, open your mouth and enunciate your words. Mumbling (remember all those freshmen rhetoric students who muttered and stammered their way through their first speech) can suggest evasiveness; those of you who are fast-talkers, slow down.

Formal Dining Situations

"Food Glorious Food." For most interview dinners, you might as well change those lyrics from the musical Oliver to "Food Laborious Food." Sometimes the interview dinner is the hardest part. It's a perfect storm of small talk, tasks, alcohol, body language, research and teaching discussions. Sometimes, you get stuck going to dinner with the most obnoxious people, and sometimes, you have a great group. By the time dinner rolls around, you're about ready to pass out. Now, you have to engage for another three hours and with a glass of wine. Well, let's start there: to drink or not to drink. That is the question. While having a drink after a long interview day might sound like a wonderful thing, if you're already running on fumes, think about the effects of alcohol on your system. If you pose a high risk for becoming quickly intoxicated because you didn't drink anything but coffee all day and those pesky grad students had you talking all through lunch, our advice, don't do it. If, on the other hand, everyone is having a glass of wine, and you can handle it, go for it. Just don't order the most expensive glass. You may also have to pay for that yourself, too. Some state funded and even private colleges have no-alcohol policies. Dining situations during on-campus visits are often important engagements during the interview process. Food is a wonderful way to reduce the amount of stress during the interview, but when faced with a formal dining situation, will you have what it takes to seal the deal, or will an embarrassing food faux-pas send you back to campus without an offer?

PhD students need to brush up on their dining skills so they can focus on getting a job, rather than getting the bone out of their mouth.

The dinner venue may be 5-star or something much less. One thing is certain; you'll not know the menu ahead of time. The menu may be one that can challenge even the most astute gastronomes. Should you pass the bread? It's right in front of you. Should you pass to the left or right? It seems so simple...but most people have never really thought about passing left or right. What about my fork? Leave it on the plate when I'm finished? I just noticed, my napkin is still on the table. There goes the job.... After the first course, you'll need to tackle an avian with an attitude as you eat bone-in chicken served with devilish angel-hair pasta and precocious peas. As a reward for the epicurean challenges, you may cautiously consume coffee with custard. Sounds like a mouthful...it is.

> *"The interview meal seems like it should be a no-brainer. It's really quite unfortunate how many PhDs are not prepared for this part of the conversation. Know your manners. It will help you relax and present yourself as a sophisticated individual."*
>
> ~Associate Dean, College of Engineering

Once seated, the best advice, according to Dee Hurst, certified etiquette expert, is to observe your host and other professionals at the table. When in doubt, their guidance can help you avoid common mistakes. When seated, take your napkin and place it in your lap. Do not order the most expensive item, nor ask for courses that are not offered to you by your host (appetizers, desserts, wine). Be careful to ask for recommendations: what if the chair recommends something that you absolutely hate: awkward! Watch out for expensive special orders. A high maintenance reputation is not the impression you want to leave. If you have food allergies, try to manage them discreetly without making too much of a fuss. Most campus hosts will not consider food allergies as they make your arrangements. Don't order something you've never had or something difficult to eat. Be courteous to the wait staff and make sure you contribute to the conversation with people on your right and left side. Be aware of conversation topics, tone and volume. The interview meal is less about the food and more about your goal of building a positive relationship with search committee members. Focus on the conversation. You will eat again.

The interview meal is less about the food and more about your goal of building a positive relationship with this potential employer. You *will* eat again, so focus on the conversation. Make conversation.

Do not begin eating until everyone at your table has been served. If there is a delay, that person will usually encourage the others to begin. Try to pace yourself so you're not done with your meal before everyone else. In general, most of us might be so nervous (and hungry) that we'll rush. *Slow down* and enjoy the dining experience. Cut only one bite at a time, and break and butter your bread one small piece at a time. Do not season your food before tasting it, and when asked, pass the salt and pepper together. Avoid asking for any condiments that are not provided with the meal. You may put catsup on your prime rib at home, but the chef would prefer that you not do it at a four star restaurant.

If something is presented that you cannot eat, just avoid it and concentrate on the other items. All items are passed to the right for the first rotation. After that, you will pass in the direction closest to that person who is requesting the item. If you are closest to an item, you are responsible for passing it along. You may offer to the person on your left before taking the item, or you may directly pass it to the person on your right. Do not turn your wine glass or coffee cup upside down, or move any of your dishes. If you wish to decline an item, quietly state, *no thank you*. Most importantly, do not talk with food in your mouth. This mistake is a deal-breaker, and prevalent in a multi-tasking generation where meetings, emails and phone calls intersect with dining. Be very conscious of this mistake. Slow down and take smaller bites. Doggie bags are never requested. Double check on your posture, and be sure to place utensils in a rest position frequently. No used utensils will ever go on the table or into a shared dish.

Formal place-setting roadmap

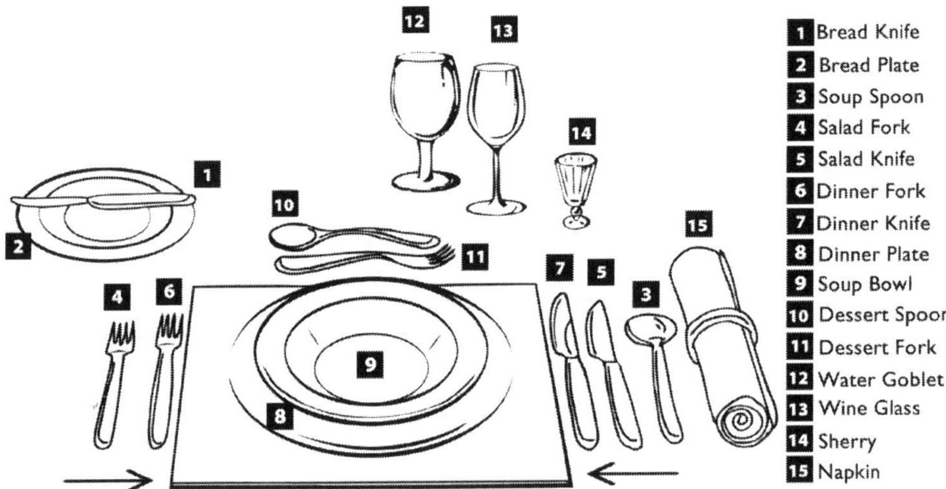

Indicate that you are completed with your course by placing your utensils across the right side of your plate diagonally. Napkins will not return to the table until you are leaving the table. If you are still conversing, the napkin remains on your lap. Wait staff do not want help lifting or moving dishes. Once finished, leave the items alone and simply concentrate on the conversation. Be sure that you thank your hosts for their hospitality. The bill is usually taken care of by the search committee, but you should have sufficient cash with you just in case. Even though it may be difficult, try hard during dinner to really listen to people, to smile, and to enjoy their company. Sure, you have lots on your mind, but remember this is one opportunity where your colleagues want to get a glimpse of who you are as a future colleague and, dare we say, friend.

Interview Questions

The old saying, *practice makes perfect*, applies just as much to learning to ride a bike as it does to preparing for an academic interview. Some candidates spend a great deal of time preparing for the minutia, focusing on the dissertation, and making sure their suit fits, all the while forgetting how far practicing interview questions might take them. Have you ever met a *know-it-all* in your field? Frankly, academe is full of them. And while you may be an emerging top scholar in your field, it's unbelievable how you might respond during the pressure of a phone interview or an on-campus visit. Don't let a know-it-all attitude prevent you from taking time to prepare: trust us, there are many questions to anticipate.

> *"I have to ask certain questions so I can know what kind of teacher you'll be. My questions will help me figure out if you are a good fit for our students, department, college, discipline and community."*
> ~Professor of Public Health, Chair Faculty Search

Before we go into the type of interview questions you can expect, let's talk about interview ethics. If you've read the *CV Handbook* by Coghill-Behrends and Anthony, you'll remember our little talk about the importance of integrity while job searching. It's so important, that we need to bring it up one more time. Honesty during the academic job search is imperative. Consider your career GAME OVER if you're caught embellishing the truth. Colleges and universities are under greater pressure and scrutiny than ever to make sure that the folks they're hiring are who they say they are. After a series of scandals in the early years of the new millennia you can be pretty certain that just about every detail of your application materials – from dates to deeds – will be double checked by someone. I'll never forget what one wise faculty member told us all in a first-year seminar, "If you crawl out on that branch, someone is going to cut it off." Don't go there. There are some trees you just shouldn't climb, and don't forget, academics get paid to be meticulous.

> *"Even the smallest exaggeration can hint of a dishonest individual."*
> ~Director of Affirmative Action Programs & Professor of Art

Interview Questions You can Expect

We could easily list 100 questions for you to think about but if you can't answer two key questions, you probably won't need to practice the other 98. These are simply questions you need to nail!

#1. Your dissertation:

- How did you choose your dissertation topic? What research tools and methodologies did you employ? What were the results? What are possible future directions or ramifications of your research? What publications have resulted or are in progress? What are the limitations of your method or of your analysis?

#2. Your teaching/research interests and experience:

- Tell me about your teaching/research experiences. How have your experiences shaped the work that you do? What is your teaching philosophy? What is your research agenda? What specific courses can you teach immediately? What does your future teaching and research agenda look like? What is your scholarship/research plan? (What will you need to be successful: technology, laboratory space, start-up funds, subjects?) What are the prospects for external funding in your area?

All applicants for academic and professional positions can expect to encounter a number of questions that are fairly predictable. Knowing that you will be quizzed, interrogated, and cross-examined should make interview-question preparation a no-brainer. It's not optional.

Our advice: become a good storyteller. Practice your interview answers in a mirror and remember to smile with your eyes, smile while answering your interview questions. Don't be so caught up in the seriousness of the moment or your answer that you come off as an academic robot. Be as personable as you can possibly be while answering interview questions. Practicing in a mirror, or in the company of others, will help you feel more prepared when you really do sit down in front of the entire search committee. Be mindful of your body language and posture. Leaning forward or sitting on the edge of your seat communicates sincere interest and attention to the interview team. Slouching back or taking a position of too much confidence seems disrespectful given your audience.

50 Common Interview Questions

1. Why is this position of interest to you?
2. Tell us about yourself.
3. What in your background will help you make a special contribution to our students, our department, our college?
4. In what ways does your teaching philosophy fit with the mission and goals of our college?
5. Describe your current research interests.
6. What do you need from us to implement your research agenda?
7. Talk to us about your view of collaboration.
8. Tell us about your service agenda.
9. How do your service areas and research intersect?
10. Tell us about your laboratory needs. What will you need to be productive?
11. Why did you decide to pursue a doctorate in this field?
12. Talk to us about funding opportunities and what role you plan on playing in grant proposals.
13. How did you choose your dissertation topic?
14. Talk to us about how you will use your dissertation for publications.
15. Describe the courses you could teach immediately and then discuss courses you would like to design for future years.
16. What are your plans for research?
17. How will you involve students in your research?
18. What was the essence of your research?
19. What do you require in order to pursue your research?
20. Where have you published your results? Where would you like to publish in the future?
21. What papers are in process?
22. How do you propose to balance teaching and research?
23. What do you see as the basic function of undergraduate education?
24. What do you see as the main contribution of this department to the overall goals of the institution?
25. Elaborate on pedagogical changes that are happening in your field or anticipated changes.
26. Talk to us about the types of community and interdisciplinary partnerships you've experienced.
27. Describe the experiences you have had with defining student learning outcomes and assessing them?
28. Explain specifically how you incorporate the concept of diversity into your classes.
29. Describe experiences with distance learning? What online tools are you most familiar?

30. What courses are you interested in teaching?
31. What was the biggest challenge you faced as a teaching assistant?
32. Are today's grades a good indication of students' academic achievement?
33. How would your undergraduate (graduate) students describe you? How would you describe them?
34. How do you help your students create work-life balance? In what ways do you help them understand time-management and good student habits?
35. What is your understanding of the mission of our College?
36. In what ways will you bring the insights of your research to your courses at the undergraduate level?
37. Tell us what ways you will implement student-success initiatives in your position as an assistant professor.
38. How do you identify students' needs in your area and how do you meet them in and out of class? Give specific examples.
39. In the courses that you taught as a TA, name one thing that students learned that was of lasting value.
40. Tell us about your past experiences with advising students regarding course load and course options. How do you see your role as an advisor in this department/college?
41. Describe your process of how student work is evaluated in your classes. How do you assist all learners in your classes?
42. What experiences have you had with first-generation college students? What teaching methods have proved effective with diverse students?
43. Tell us about the professional development activities you need for continued success in your field.
44. As you know from our mission statement, our institution is committed to community service. How can you support that mission?
45. How do you view the relevance of your research area/teaching area in today's changing educational landscape? What changes do you anticipate in the future?
46. In what ways will the infusion of technology change your teaching?
47. How will you recruit talented students to your program area?
48. In what ways do you see your research making a difference for the community at large? How will you contribute to the community?
49. Do you see any significant challenges of this position with what you have learned so far during your on-campus visit? How would you meet these challenges? What resources would you need to adequately address them?
50. How would you contribute to the improvement/growth of our department (college)?

Interview Topics

In addition to the interview questions we've provided, spend some time thinking about how you might approach some of the broad interview topics that are common at academic interviews. Because each faculty member will ask questions in a particular way, thinking about interview questions in broader topic-form will be to your advantage. Plan to have something definitive to say about each of these topics if they relate to you or the position. Here are topics that may be important for you to review:

Interview topics:

Instructional strategies	Teaching experiences	Teaching interests
Course development	Writing and publishing	Technology applications
Technology integration	Student success initiatives	Presentations & Workshops
Research agenda	Academic background	Philosophy and beliefs
Statistical applications	Professional goals	Previous experiences
Assessment strategies	Online learning	Standards and ethics
Professional strengths	Grant writing	Areas of expertise
Academic accomplishments	Collaborative projects	Research funding
Service/outreach and leadership	Legislative factors/initiatives	Laboratory protocol
Assessment	Future projects	Advising

Inappropriate Questions

Anyone preparing for an interview should be aware that federal and state guidelines have been established regarding the type of information which can be requested. Questions regarding race, religion, or national origin are always inappropriate; other questions may be considered potentially discriminatory and are inappropriate unless they are asked of each applicant. Because the interviewers you will encounter are seldom personnel specialists, it is quite possible that some inappropriate questions may be raised innocently with no intent to discriminate. Federal laws prohibit employers from asking questions that are discriminatory.

> *"Even in this day and age, candidates need to be ready for the inappropriate question about something personal. It might be about the person's spouse, or children, or origin of their name. Individuals on search committees have been informed about what's acceptable and what is not acceptable in regards to interview questions."*
>
> ~Affirmative Action Director

You don't have to try to figure out what the interviewer has in mind. In the first place, you don't have time and second, you have a 50 percent chance of being wrong. Rather than trying to second-guess the interviewer, it's a good idea to have thought about the types of inappropriate questions and to have an idea of how you will handle them. Whatever the questioner's intention may be, you are not obligated to answer the following questions:

Are you married? What is your spouse's/partner's occupation?

Do you have children? Are you pregnant?

Where do your parents live and what do they do for a living?

When and where were you born?

Do you have a disability?

Have you ever been treated for a mental or emotional problem?

Have you ever been arrested?

What is your religious affiliation?

What is your native language?

What type of military discharge did you receive?

One caution: sometimes questions border on the inappropriate and are genuinely not intended to offend, especially if you're really connecting well with your campus hosts. We do strongly encourage you to think about what kinds of inappropriate questions you could be asked and rehearse ahead of time some diplomatic responses. Whether you see these questions as unnerving, frustrating, or even amusing, if you have prepared for the possibility of encountering inappropriate or discriminatory questions, you will be able to respond without intimidation, discomfiting embarrassment, or guilt.

Questions for the Search Committee

Depending upon the interview structure and format, you may not have the opportunity to ask questions of your own until the interview is nearly finished. Although interviewers expect that you will have some questions to ask of them, not all will set aside time for this purpose. Even those who do invite questions often wait until they have covered all of the topics they consider most important. It is natural that you will formulate questions during the course of the interview, but you should also have prepared some general questions covering topics of special interest to you. The nature and timing of your questions will demonstrate that you have given some thought to the position, that you have listened attentively as the conversation progressed, and that you are sincerely interested in making the right decision.

Questions can be used to clarify ambiguities or to gather information about topics not covered. Developing your questions in advance will help you to avoid two potentially negative or embarrassing possibilities: asking questions simply for the sake of asking questions or drawing a blank when the opportunity arises.

Questions about Teaching

Most of you will have some teaching responsibilities in the new job. Have the various individuals with whom you have met addressed the following?

Course load	Course release	Online teaching
Course materials	Course evaluations	Student profile
Attrition rate	Advising responsibilities	Summer teaching
Teaching assistants	Joint appointments	Grading policies
Technology	Other media resources	Course sequencing

Having specifics in mind about teaching load and evaluations will make you a more perceptive interviewee, and, will give you the material to make a wise decision should an offer be made.

Questions about Research

If you are seeking a position at a research extensive university, research activity and productivity is required. To be successful, you'll need basic information to help you analyze whether the institution's resources and infrastructure are adequate for your particular area of research. The following topics should be covered:

Budget	Research expectations	Equipment
Start-up funds	Personnel	Supplies
Patent policies	Laboratory space	Research facilities
Research assistants	Conference monies	Collaborations
Grant expectations	Publication requirements	Technology/software

Questions about Tenure

Timing and tact is everything in an interview. How do you talk about tenure when you haven't been offered the job? Basically, you talk about the topics involved in the tenure process with diplomacy. Bringing these topics up in conversation, rather than in a questioning mode, will probably get you most of the answers you need. The person who should be asked about any tenure-related questions is the top administrator in the College, typically the Dean.

Process	Guidelines	Tenure clock
Timeline	Reviewers	Support
Writing support	Dossier requirements	Annual reviews

Picking up on Conversational Cues

Don't talk yourself out of a job. It's not your responsibility as an applicant to fill every silence, especially with chitchat. Avoid asking too many questions in an effort to fill the silence. Never initiate conversation about unrelated topics, and don't dominate the conversation. Silence is far less harmful. Are you watching for interview closure clues? It's important to recognize the interviewer's signals about concluding the interview. It's a fatal mistake to prolong the meeting. Some closure clues are easy to recognize: shuffling papers; putting your CV into a folder; pushing a chair back; cleaning their glasses again and again (changing contacts with no solution); disruptive coughing; and thanking you one more time for coming to the interview.

Don't talk yourself out of a job. Saying too much is probably worse than saying too little. Watch your audience for signs of coma. You don't want to put anyone to sleep, but you also don't want to annoy them either.

If you don't catch on to the interview-ending clues, one of the faculty members may stand up, prompting others to follow. Be alert and be ready to thank all of the members around the table for their time. Be professional and also indicate your interest in being considered for the position. It's always appropriate to show that kind of sincere interest.

Interview Follow Up: Evaluating your Interview Performance

No interview is complete without your evaluation. Whether you are waiting in a campus lounge, motel room, or airport terminal, the period immediately following the interview should be used productively. While everything is fresh in your mind, try to make some notes about important topics covered and be sure to jot down items that should have been discussed or questions you should have asked but didn't because there was insufficient time or because you simply forgot.

This is not the time to speculate on your chances of being hired. Incorrect speculations can lead to greater disappointments and letdowns and may affect your preparation and performance at future interviews. You cannot compare yourself with other candidates interviewed; nor, can you know all the factors that influence the ultimate selection of the person to be hired. Consequently, it is pointless to attempt predictions. The only speculation you should make is whether you would accept the position if offered.

The post-interview evaluation period should be a time for retrospection.

The post-interview evaluation period should be a time for positive retrospection. Being overly critical of yourself or of the interviewer serves no useful purpose and results in a loss of objectivity. One of the easiest things for you to evaluate is your response to specific questions. If you stumbled or could not come up with a satisfactory answer, focus your attention on these problem areas before your next interview. Also, think about those questions you answered well. Note your responses and hope that you will be asked similar questions in future interviews.

Not all interviews result in a job offer. Don't take it personally.

Reflecting on how you conducted yourself during social functions in interview situations should also be a priority in a post-interview evaluation. Many of your reactions will depend upon your hosts. If they take the initiative to introduce you to others and make sure that you feel comfortable, group functions are more manageable than if you are left to circulate on your own. You should not depend on your host to act as a liaison, however. Be prepared to step out on your own, to introduce yourself, and to chat with as many guests as possible.

After the Interview	
GOALS:	• Know how the timeline for decision-making fits into your personal calendar if other campus visits are scheduled or if you're waiting for other offers.
HOMEWORK:	• Reflect on the interview – positives and negatives. Send a thank-you to host(s) right away. • Prepare accepting/rejecting statements. • Compare competing offers – side-by-side and consider your personal and professional needs inventories when making decisions.

The Offer

You've just gotten home from a whirlwind tour of Big State University. You're ready to relax, to sleep, and to spend time with your loved ones. Your interview consumes your mind. Did you read the faculty at Big State University right? It seemed like they really liked you, you think they really were interested in your research. The Dean seemed impressed with both your track record of securing funding and the promise for more external funding in the future. You related well with the undergrad and graduate students in the department. They liked your ideas for courses, for new initiatives to connect the students to some populations with whom you've worked. You've just hung up your suit and are ready to watch your favorite sitcom when your phone rings. You've been waiting for this moment for days…and the area code that pops up is one that you recognize: it's the chair of the search committee, and she has good news.

The final component of any job search is accepting an offer of employment. Simple as this seems, every job seeker needs to be aware that offers can be extended in different ways and that there are many decisions to be made before an offer should be accepted. Receiving an offer marks the culmination of your efforts; it can also spur a brief but intense period of soul-searching as well as celebration. For most academics and professionals, the decision to accept or reject an offer of employment has far-reaching consequences. Accepting the offer represents both a legal and ethical commitment that should not be entered into without careful consideration of the effect of the decision on your immediate plans and your future objectives.

It's most likely you'll receive a phone call, but occasionally an offer comes via email. Remember to check your email and voicemail regularly when you are waiting for an offer. Employment offers always require a response and the individual extending the offer will typically indicate a deadline for your acceptance. This initial phone call usually won't address salary or the terms of the offer; don't bring it up either. They'll send you that in an offer letter or email.

Most committees will expect a relatively immediate response. Some candidates think too hard about the initial offer. A few of you will have multiple offers on the table. Some of you will be in the precarious situation of getting an offer before you've gone to your last campus interview. It's a tough situation for sure. Our advice: if you get an offer that you want, accept it verbally as soon as possible.

Don't play mind games with your future colleagues.
Getting the job offer is hard work. Accepting it is the easy part.

There are no rules or gold standards regarding how the offer, negotiations, and contract-signing process are handled. Most departments have done their homework in advance of the offer they extend to you by checking in: what do you need to be successful here? We're planning to offer the following starting salary. Is this agreeable to you? Your teaching and research expectations are the following…you get our point. Rarely, does an offer arrive as a complete surprise. Again: accept notification of an offer with a smile and a handshake. They want you. It's a good feeling.

Elements of an Offer

Offers will vary depending on the type and the title of the position (faculty, professional staff, administrative), position responsibilities (tenure-track, clinical, instructional, research), and institutional identity (research extensive, liberal arts campus, community college, etc.). There are some details that will always be spelled out in an offer, including: position title, rank, and starting date; workload expectations; salary and benefits; and opportunities for support. Take a look at the following list of elements of an offer that might be critical in your decision-making process. Some items are fixed and non-negotiable.

Rank & Salary	Lab/Office Space	Teaching Load
Assistantships	Research Funding	Tuition Remission
Tenure Clock	Research Budget	Travel Budget
Association Fees	Extra Duties/Service	Spousal Assistance
Course Release	Sabbatical/Leave Policy	House Hunting Trip
Parental Leave Policy	Office Supports	Technology
Appointment & Classification	Relocation/Moving Assistance	Summer Opportunities

Sample Contract Offer Letter

Office of the Provost
Big State University
Anyplace, Any State, Zip

April 1, 201x

Will B. Goode, Ph.D.
21 College Street
Anyplace, Any State, Zip

Dear Dr. Goode:

The Big State University is pleased to offer you a tenure-track faculty position in the College of Liberal Arts and Sciences. This letter will outline both the financial terms and scholarly obligations of the Assistant Professor of German position. As required by law, the university is conducting a credential check of your academic and professional background. Your appointment is contingent on successful verification.

Your position is a full-time academic year appointment with a first-year salary of $83,200.00. The University has a comprehensive benefits package in addition to your salary which is fully disclosed at: www.bigstateuniversity.edu/faculty. Big State University newly appointed faculty are provided with a three-year appointment, beginning August 201x and ending June 201x. Reviews occur annually and reappointments are made during the third year unless you receive official notification that the third year is a terminal year. Review for tenure and promotion will occur during the 201x-201x year. Big State University renewals are based on an evaluation of scholarship, teaching or creative work, and service to the college and the profession. Big State's Tenure Guidebook is outlined at: www.bigstateuniversity.edu/tenure. After a successful third-year review, you may request a one-semester reduction in teaching load to more fully pursue your research program.

As a new tenure-track appointment, you will be assigned a mentor at the rank of full professor. The attached document, *Mentors at Big State*, will be a guide for both you and the mentor assigned to work with you.

The teaching load at Big State University is two courses per semester. A quarter-time teaching assistant will be provided for your first year. In addition to your teaching duties, you will be advising both undergraduate, Master's and doctoral-level students; and, supervising graduate research. Assistant professors may be granted a Wildcat Summer Research Fellowship (WSRF) based on a proposal for research development that results in a publication or a new instructional product. The WSRF is a fixed amount ($8,000) that is added as a salary stipend from which taxes and fringe benefits will be deducted. If desired, WSRF monies may be used to support international travel that supports your research needs.

Page 2, Contract Letter

The College of Liberal Arts and Sciences supports newly appointed tenure-track faculty who participate in professional meetings by contributing to scholarly symposia or by presenting research papers. The professional development fees awarded are $1,000 for year one, two and three. Your office space, 21 Canyon Building, will be equipped with the Apple desktop system discussed at the interview, along with a classroom set (20) of the newest iPads. A $2,000.00 budget for apps will be provided through the Department.

As part of the relocation package, Big State University will provide for you and your spouse/partner, an opportunity to return to the community to seek housing. You will be provided with the equivalent of airfare (round-trip tickets), two nights in the Campus Hotel, and a $60.00 per diem to cover food or miscellaneous expenses. In addition, Big State works with World-wide Mover and, upon acceptance of this offer, you will be contacted by the university finance officer to arrange reimbursement for your expenses (maximum amount of $5,000.00). Please review the moving policy at: www.bigstateuniversity.edu/moving

Your appointment commences on August 20, 201x, at a college-wide orientation for new faculty. Orientation begins at 9:00am in the Boulder Building (221) and is conducted by the University Benefits Office. At this meeting, all details of your benefits plan and your flex benefits plan will be addressed. The Provost's Office conducts a new faculty orientation at 1:00pm on Monday, August 20th. All new faculty are required to attend both orientation sessions. A reception will be held in the Mouflon Room of the University Museum at 7:00pm. A detailed itinerary will be forwarded to you regarding these meetings and additional meetings scheduled in your college and department.

Big State University is a highly regarded institution of higher learning and we are looking forward to your scholarly contributions to our students and our college. Our deadline for acceptance of this offer of employment is on or before April 13, 201x. To accept this offer, please complete the following and return via certified mail to the address stated below. Should you have questions, please call Associate Provost, Dr. Mei Kann at 398.876.0976.

Sincerely,

B.F. Deall

Provost B.F. Deall

My signature below confirms my acceptance of this offer of employment:

Signature: ______________________________

Date: ______________________________

Return to:
Provost B.F. Deall, Boulder Building, Suite 783
Big State University, Anyplace, Anywhere, State 12689

Considering the College

Once you receive an offer of employment, there are a number of personal and professional items that you will want to address. Some advisors will encourage you to take your time, think about it, make sure it is the best you can get considering the current job market. One thought that most mentors won't talk about: you (the job seeker) are more emotionally invested in the job search and more likely to panic or react when hearing good (or sadly bad) news. Of course you are in the middle of it while they are cheerleading on the sidelines. They are an invaluable resource for sure, but you have to make the ultimate decision based on what you know and what you feel. Yep – trust your instincts. Consideration of the following questions may influence your decision to accept or decline an offer:

- Is this the kind of job I want?
- Do I feel comfortable with other faculty/staff/administrators?
- Is my philosophy compatible with that of the institution?
- Are research facilities adequate and accessible?
- Are salary and benefits satisfactory?
- Is the institution financially sound?
- Are there interdisciplinary research opportunities?
- Am I capable of the teaching/research load?
- Can I function independently to make tenure?
- Are they offering supports to help my spouse/partner find work?

Considering your Career

You will also need to consider the effects of the offered position on your career by attempting to answer the following questions:

- Will I be working in my area of expertise?
- Does the position support my professional development?
- Is there opportunity for advancement/promotion?
- Could this be a stepping stone to a better job?
- Is the organization/institution reputable?
- Can I find personal as well as professional satisfaction in the job?

Considering the Community

The position, the terms of appointment, and the institution or organization are primary considerations for everyone. But if you receive more than one offer or if you must consider the needs and desires of other family members, the features of the community must also be evaluated. Your consideration of the community should be less about what you think you know about a certain place and more about whether you can imagine living, surviving, socializing, and thriving in a given place. For example, when we say Florida, folks begin to think of all sorts of things (water, Disney, alligators). You do know that there are places in Florida where you'd find none of those things, right? Questions you will need to consider might include:

- Is housing available and affordable?
- Is transportation/commuting convenient?
- Are there employment/educational opportunities for my spouse/partner?
- Are there satisfactory day-care facilities/schools for my children?
- Do community recreational/cultural resources meet my needs?
- What's the safety and crime record in the area?
- What health and community services are available? Do you, or your loved ones, have health needs that require special services, or a certain kind of climate?
- What's the cultural scene, including: fine arts venues, nightlife, sports teams and facilities, and children-friendly activities?

If you have followed through with your post-interview evaluations, you have probably already considered the various opportunities you may have and how they fit into your professional and personal goals. What were your reflections on the community? Your decision can be made quickly and without much difficulty if the offer is from your preferred institution or organization.

> *"The location, the job, and its colleagues are a whole-life decision. You need to think about where you want to work, play, socialize. We want you to be happy outside of work as well"*
>
> ~Dean, Medical School

Balancing Multiple Offers

Some candidates find themselves in the flattering position of having multiple offers to consider. In this situation, careful and honest communication is called for. It is key to remember that we work in small academic communities: word travels quickly when candidates are out and about. Once you've had a campus visit, the anonymity of your candidacy at a particular institution is, well, non-existent. The best candidates on the market will likely have multiple interviews and, if they've played their cards right, multiple offers. You, unfortunately, have little control over when your interviews will be scheduled putting some of you in the precarious situation of receiving an offer before completing all of the interviews. What should you do? The best answer is to be honest with all involved. If you've received an offer before you interview at an institution that you prefer, contact the chair of the search committee immediately and share your news. They might offer to reschedule your interview if you are their top candidate, but more often than not, they'll tell you to decide: either accept the offer, ask for more time, or kindly decline the offer and really hope that you seal the deal at the upcoming interview.

Search committees vary a great deal on how much time they are willing to give a candidate considering an offer. It's not unreasonable to ask for time to consider, but we caution about sending the wrong message to the folks who are potentially your future colleagues. Nobody likes feeling like second best. Your advisor can be a great resource during this time, and many advisors like being in the loop. They'll likely have insight into the departments (maybe even other candidates who are interviewing) and therefore, better able to give you sound advice on whether offers are reasonable, or whether you should decline and continue interviewing. Because each situation is so sensitive and unique, we strongly encourage you to know yourself: would you earnestly be interested in establishing your career where you've received the offer? What does your advisor think about your situation and the market? About the offer? About your upcoming interviews? Is passing up the initial offer worth the risks? It's never a good idea to make a hasty decision, nor is it a good idea to sell yourself short. One to two weeks is a comfortable request for additional time. Asking for more time than two weeks is sending a very clear message to the search committee that you either have other interviews, are consider other offers, or that you're not that interested in committing to them. Proceed with caution.

Negotiations

The negotiations process is started long before you are invited to a campus interview. Think about your priorities ahead of the interview. Know what is important to you; in fact, know your top priorities so that you can be successful in your new career. When an offer is made, you'll be able to talk about your needs in a manner that is both comfortable and professional. Winning negotiations is typically a result of knowing what you need and what your field can afford. Some individuals get so hung up on more money that they lose sight of the bigger more important picture: what do I need to be successful?

> *"Know your market. Some of you are in fields where there is high demand and few qualified applicants. In this case you might have a bit more negotiating pull. Some of you are in areas in which there are many candidates and few openings—the market will pay accordingly."*
>
> ~Dean, College of Letters

Sometimes the offer is right on the mark: everything you were hoping for with a reasonable salary to boot. And sometimes, a candidate will negotiate to get something that they'll need to be a productive faculty member. To help you better understand the process, and more importantly, to ensure the negotiations process is productive, rather than problematic, here is a simple device to help you stay on track – just remember this: negotiations are all about being OPEN: knowing the *Offer*, *Place*, *Expectations*, and your *Needs*. This philosophy should guide not only your attention but also your demeanor. Throughout the negotiations process, consider your tact:

- **Demonstrate flexibility**
  Am I understanding the resources that are being offered?
- **Demonstrate confidence not arrogance**
  Am I making reasonable requests of my future colleagues?
- **Demonstrate a commitment to be successful**
  Am I communicating an interest in being a team player in the department?
- **Demonstrate an investment to students**
  How will these things I need help my students and my research?

Your negotiations team is made up of your advisors, colleagues, and even search committee members, particularly the Chair. Yep, the Chair of your search is probably your biggest advocate and *ace in your hand*, because at the point an offer has been extended, they're ready to do all it takes to bring you to campus (within reason). Carefully discuss the details of your offer with your advisor. Engage in frank and open discussion with the Chair about the terms of the offer. The hiring institution has already invested lots in you. Chances are, if your requests are reasonable and well-intentioned, you might just get what you ask for.

What's Negotiable?

The non-negotiables will vary by institution, and most of you will know intuitively what's up for discussion and what's off limits, like rank, advising responsibilities, and research expectations. If something in the offer doesn't meet your expectations (salary, course load) you may have some, but not much wiggle room. Again, check with your advisor about what's reasonable. If you find language in the letter that is surprising or unexpected, contact the search chair for clarification. Lastly, if you are curious about options for employment for significant others, the department chair is the best person to contact and start the conversation about the resources and supports available to new faculty hires who are relocating with companions.

The Chair of the search is your advocate and ally, not your adversary.

If you need additional research costs covered, ask for it in a way that communicates your desire to be a productive member of the department. It's important to make sure you have some basis for a negotiable item. Let's take the one that gets the most attention: salary. If you request a higher salary (and by higher we're not talking much more than $5,000 typically) you really must be able to demonstrate:

1. The salaries at comparable institutions are higher;
2. You have another offer on the table with a higher starting salary;
3. You have a record or high likelihood of bringing in significant external funding that would benefit the college financially;
4. The offer is lower than what you're currently making.

Do you see how asking for a higher salary for the sake of making more money without some sort of reasonable rationale comes across as demanding? Some institutions simply can't play in the sandbox given the financial squeeze on higher ed. The PhD planner on the topic is a great place to start.

Saying Thanks

You've just won the Oscar for best new faculty hire. You have a minute to thank everyone who's helped you get this far: from your third grade teacher who turned you onto your obscure field, to your dissertation advisor and mentor, to your family and friends who stuck with you through the difficult process of writing a dissertation, job seeking, and now preparing for a major move.

One of the most important things to remember in this entire process is that none of us are truly capable of going it all alone. We find inspiration from our peers, from our advisors, from our parents, and from all sorts of individuals along the way. You did it. It was your hard work that got you here, but be a good human and remember to pay special thanks to those who were committed to your success. After you've received and accepted an offer, don't forget to send a note of thanks to your new soon-to-be-colleagues. They, in many ways, were the final group that believed in you and pushed you to the top of the summit. They are looking forward to working with you. Let them know that you, too, are excited about the future. In just a short while you will become an advisor, a faculty member, and a mentor to students. Embody those qualities in your advisors, mentors, and teachers that helped you succeed, and pass them on to the next generation of scholars. Congratulations. Pay it forward.

Notes

Notes

Professional Associations

Professional Associations and Organizations

Professional associations play a key role in the advancement of most disciplines. Faculty, institutions, departments, even individual graduate students can become members of some. It's imperative that you are completely familiar with the primary and even some secondary organizations and associations that are important in your discipline. Of course, many of these associations use their president's or chief officer's campus as a host for a term period. For this reason, contact information, leadership, and web addresses change on a regular basis. Google the association name or discuss with your colleagues to locate an association that's moved. As of 2012, the associations and organizations listed below provided the following information.

ARTS & COMMUNICATION

Accrediting Council on Education in Journalism and Mass Communication
University of Kansas, School of Journalism,
1435 Jayhawk Boulevard, Stauffer-Flint Hall
Lawrence, KS 66045-7575
(785) 864-3973
www2.ku.edu/~acejmc/

American Choral Directors Association
545 Couch Drive
Oklahoma City OK 73102-2207
(405) 232-8161
acda.org/

American Council for the Arts
(now called Americans for the Arts)
Washington DC office: 1000 Vermont Avenue, NW, 6th Floor
Washington, DC 20005
(202) 371-2830
New York City office: One East 53rd Street, 2nd Floor
New York, NY 10022
(212) 223-2787
www.artsusa.org/

American Musicological Society
6010 College Station
Brunswick ME 04011-8451
(207) 798-4243
www.ams-net.org/

American Society for Theatre Research
PO Box 1798
Boulder, CO 80306-1798
(303) 530-1838 or (888) 530-1838
www.astr.org/

American String Teachers Association
4155 Chain Bridge Road
Fairfax, VA 22030
(703) 279-2113
www.astaweb.com/

Association for Educational Communications and Technology
P.O. Box 2447
Bloomington, IN 47402-2447
(877) 677-AECT or (812) 335-7675
www.aect.org/

Association for Theatre in Higher Education
P.O. Box 1290
Boulder, CO 80306-1290
(888) 284-3737 or (303) 530-2167
www.athe.org

Association of Performing Arts Presenters
1211 Connecticut Avenue NW, Suite 200
Washington, DC 20036
(888) 820-ARTS (2787) or (202) 833-2787
www.artspresenters.org

Association of Teachers of Technical Writing
www.attw.org/

Broadcast Education Association
1771 N Street NW
Washington, DC 20036
(202) 429-5355
www.beaweb.org/

College Art Association
50 Broadway, 21st Floor
New York, NY 10004
(212) 691-1051
www.collegeart.org/

College Media Association
Vanderbilt University
2301 Vanderbilt Place
VU Station B 351669
Nashville, TN 37235-1669
(615) 322-6610
www.collegemedia.org

College Music Society
312 East Pine Street
Missoula, MT 59802
(406) 721-9616
www.music.org/

Conference on College Composition and Communication
1111 W. Kenyon Road
Urbana, IL 61801-1096
(217) 328-3870
www.ncte.org/cccc

Congress on Research in Dance
3416 Primm Lane
Birmingham, AL 35216
(205) 823-5517
www.cordance.org/

Council for Interior Design Accreditation (formerly FIDER)
206 Grandville Ave., Suite 350
Grand Rapids, MI 49503
(616) 458-0400
www.accredit-id.org

Council of Colleges of Arts and Sciences
The College of William and Mary
P.O. Box 8795
Williamsburg, VA 23187-8795
(757) 221-1784
www.ccas.net

Educational Theatre Association
2343 Auburn Avenue
Cincinnati, OH 45219-2815
(513) 421-3900
www.edta.org/

Intercollegiate Broadcasting System, Inc.
367 Windsor Highway
New Windsor, NY 12553
(845) 565-0003
www.ibsradio.org/

International Communication Association
1500 21st Street, NW
Washington, DC 20036
(202) 955-1444
www.icahdq.org/

International Society for the Performing Arts
630 9th Avenue, Suite 213
New York, NY 10036-4752
(212) 206-8490
www.ispa.org/

Linguistic Society of America
1325 18th St. NW #211
Washington, DC 20036-6501
(202) 835-1714
www.lsadc.org/

Music Educators National Conference
(now called The National Association for Music Education)
1806 Robert Fulton Drive
Reston, VA 20191
(703) 860-4000 or (800) 336-3768
www.menc.org/

Music Teachers National Association
441 Vine St., Suite 3100
Cincinnati, OH 45202-3004
(513) 421-1420 or (888) 512-5278
www.mtna.org/

National Art Education Association
1806 Robert Fulton Drive, Suite 300
Reston, VA 20191-1590
(703) 860-8000
www.naea-reston.org/

National Association of College Wind and Percussion Instructors
308 Hillcrest Drive
Kirksville, MO 63501
(660) 665-2558
nacwpi.org/

National Association of Schools of Art and Design
11250 Roger Bacon Drive, Suite 21
Reston, VA 20190-5248
(703) 437-0700
nasad.arts-accredit.org/

National Association of Schools of Dance
11250 Roger Bacon Drive, Suite 21
Reston, VA 20190-5248
(703) 437-0700
nasd.arts-accredit.org/

National Association of Schools of Music
11250 Roger Bacon Drive, Suite 21
Reston, VA 20190-5248
(703) 437-0700
nasm.arts-accredit.org/

National Association of Schools of Theatre
11250 Roger Bacon Drive, Suite 21
Reston, VA 20190-5248
(703) 437-0700
nast.arts-accredit.org/

National Association of Teachers of Singing
9957 Moorings Drive, Suite 401
Jacksonville, FL 32257
(904) 992-9101
www.nats.org/

National Communication Association
1765 N Street, NW
Washington DC 20036
(202) 464-4622
www.natcom.org/

National Dance Association
1900 Association Dr.
Reston, VA 20191-1598
(703) 476-3400 or (800) 213-7193
www.aahperd.org/nda/

Society for Ethnomusicology
www.ethnomusicology.org/

Southern States Communication Association
www.ssca.net/

University Film and Video Association
www.ufva.org/

University Photographers' Association of America
Moraine Valley Community College
9000 W. College Parkway
Palos Hills, IL 60465
(708) 974-5495
www.upaa.org/

COUNSELING & HUMAN SERVICES

American Art Therapy Association
225 North Fairfax Street
Alexandria, VA 22314
(888) 290-0878
www.arttherapy.org/

American Association for Marriage and Family Therapy
112 South Alfred Street,
Alexandria, VA 22314-3061
(703) 838-9808
www.aamft.org/

American Association for Music Therapy, Inc.
(now the American Music Therapy Association, Inc.)
8455 Colesville Road, Suite 1000
Silver Spring, MD 20910
(301) 589-3300
www.musictherapy.org/

American College Counseling Association
5999 Stevenson Avenue
Alexandria, VA 22304-3300
www.collegecounseling.org/

American College Personnel Association
One Dupont Circle, NW, Suite 300
Washington, DC 20036
(202) 835.2272
www2.myacpa.org/au/

American Counseling Association
5999 Stevenson Ave
Alexandria, VA 22304
(800) 347-6647
www.counseling.org/

American Dance Therapy Association
Suite 108, 10632 Little Patuxent Parkway
Columbia, MD 21044-3263
(410) 997-4040
www.adta.org/

American Mental Health Counselors Association
801 N. Fairfax Street, Suite 304
Alexandria, VA 22314
(800) 326-2642 or (703) 548-6002
www.amhca.org/

American Music Therapy Association, Inc.
(formerly the American Association for Music Therapy, Inc.)
8455 Colesville Road, Suite 1000
Silver Spring, MD 20910
(301) 589-3300
www.musictherapy.org/

American Occupational Therapy Association
4720 Montgomery Lane , PO Box 31220
Bethesda, MD 20824-1220
(301) 652-2682
www.aota.org/

American Physical Therapy Association
1111 North Fairfax Street
Alexandria, VA 22314-1488
(800) 999- 2782 or (703) 684- 2782
www.apta.org/

American Psychological Association
750 First Street NE
Washington, DC 20002-4242
(800) 374-2721 or (202) 336-5500
www.apa.org/

American Rehabilitation Counseling Association
www.arcaweb.org/

American Speech-Language-Hearing Association
Council on Academic Accreditation in Audiology & Speech-Language Pathology
2200 Research Boulevard
Rockville, MD 20850-3289
(301) 296-5700
www.asha.org

Association for Adult Development and Aging
(800) 347-6647
www.aadaweb.org/

Association for Counselor Education and Supervision
5999 Stevenson Avenue
Alexandria, VA 22304
(866) 815-2237 or (703) 212-2237
www.acesonline.net/

Association for Multicultural Counseling and Development
5999 Stevenson Avenue
Alexandria, VA 22304-3300
(703) 823-9800 or (800) 347-6647
www.multiculturalcounseling.org/

College and University Professionals Association for Human Resources
1811 Commons Point Drive
Knoxville, TN 37932
(865) 637-7673 or (877) 287-2474
www.cupahr.org

Commission on Accreditation for Marriage and Family Therapy Education
American Association for Marriage and Family Therapy
112 South Alfred Street
Alexandria, VA 22314
(703) 838-9808
www.aamft.org

Council on Social Work Education
1701 Duke Street, Suite 200
Alexandria, VA 22314
(703) 683-8080
www.cswe.org

National Association for Music Therapy
(now the American Music Therapy Association, Inc.)
8455 Colesville Road, Suite 1000
Silver Spring, MD 20910
(301) 589-3300
www.musictherapy.org/

National Association of Social Workers
750 First Street, NE, Suite 700
Washington, DC 20002-4241
(202) 408-8600
www.naswdc.org/

National Council on Rehabilitation Education
1099 E. Champlain Drive, Suite A
PMB # 137
Fresno, CA 93720
(559) 906-0787
www.rehabeducators.org/

DIVERSITY RESOURCES IN HIGHER ED

American Association of Hispanics in Higher Education
http://www.aahhe.org/

Consortium of Higher Education LGBT Resource Professionals
http://www.lgbtcampus.org/

Emerging Scholars Interdisciplinary Network
Room B652, School of Social Work
University of Michigan
1080 South University Avenue
Ann Arbor, MI 48109-1106
emergingscholars.net/

Gay Lesbian Medical Association GLMA
1326 18th Street NW, Suite 22
Washington, DC 20036
(202) 600-8037
glma.org

Holmes Scholars Program
aacte.org/Programs/AACTE-Holmes-Scholars-Program/

Latinos in Higher Education
Hispanic Recruitment Services, Inc.
Latinosinhighered.com
P. O. Box 16
Cromwell, CT 06416-0016
(860) 632-7676
www.latinosinhighered.com

National Association of Holmes Scholars Alumni
Dr. Jacob Easley II
Mercy College
1200 Waters Place
Bronx, NY 10461
www.nahsa.com

EDUCATION & STUDENT SERVICES

FHI 360 *formerly* Academy for Educational Development
1825 Connecticut Avenue NW
Washington, DC 20009-5721
(202) 884-8000
www.aed.org

Accrediting Council for Continuing Education and Training
1722 N Street NW
Washington, DC 20036
(202) 955-1113
www.accet.org

Accrediting Council for Independent Colleges and Schools
750 First Street, NE, Suite 980
Washington, DC 20002-4241
(202) 336-6780
www.acics.org

Alabama Association of Independent Colleges and Universities
5950 Carmichael Place, Suite 213
Montgomery, AL 36117
(334) 356-2220
www.aaicu.net

American Academy for Liberal Education
127 S. Peyton St. Suite 210
Alexandria, VA 22314
(703) 717-9719
www.aale.org

American Association for Adult and Continuing Education
10111 Martin Luther King, Jr. Hwy, Suite 200C
Bowie, MD 20720
(301) 459-6261
http://www.aaace.org/

American Association for Employment in Education, Inc.
947 E. Johnstown Road #170
Gahanna, Ohio 43230
(614) 485-1111
www.aaee.org

American Association for Higher Education and Accreditation
2020 Pennsylvania Ave NW #975
Washington, DC 20006
(202) 293-6440 or (888) 276-1299
www.aahea.org/

American Association for Vocational Instructional Materials
220 Smithonia Road
Winterville, GA 30683
(800) 228-4689
www.aavim.com

American Association for Women in Community Colleges
1582 S. Parker Road, Suite 201
Denver, CO 80231
(801) 681-2797
www.aawccnatl.org

American Association of Colleges for Teacher Education
1307 New York Ave, NW, Suite 300
Washington, DC 20005
(202) 293-2450
aacte.org/

American Association of Collegiate Registrars & Admissions Officers
One Dupont Circle NW, Suite 520
Washington, DC 20036
(202) 293-9161
www.aacrao.org/

American Association of Community Colleges
One Dupont Circle NW, Suite 410
Washington, DC 20036
(202) 728-0200
www.aacc.nche.edu

American Association of Phonetic Sciences
PO Box 23005
St. Louis, MO 63156
(314) 293-1940
www.phoneticsciences.com

American Association of Physics Teachers
One Physics Ellipse
College Park, MD 20740-3845
(301) 209-3311
www.aapt.org

American Association of Presidents of Independent Colleges and Universities
Box 7070
Provo, UT 84602-7070
(801) 422-5624
www.apicu.org

American Association of State Colleges and Universities
1307 New York Ave., NW 5th Floor
Washington, DC 20005
(202) 293-7070
www.aascu.org

American Association of University Administrators
P.O. Box 29
Stoughton, MA 02072
(781) 752-7878
www.aaua.org

American Association of University Professors
1133 Nineteenth St., NW, Suite 200
Washington, DC 20036
(202) 737-5900
www.aaup.org/aaup

American Association of University Women
111 Sixteenth Street NW
Washington, DC 20036
(800) 326-2289
www.aauw.org

American Board of Funeral Service Education Committee on Accreditation
3414 Ashland Avenue, Suite G
St. Joseph, MO 64506
(816) 233-3747
www.abfse.org

American College Counseling Association
www.collegecounseling.org/

American College Personnel Association
One Dupont Circle, NW, Suite 300
Washington, DC 20036
(202) 835-2272
www2.myacpa.org/au/

American Collegiate Retailing Association
Sam Walton College of Business
University of Arkansas, WJWH 538
Fayette, AR 72701
(334) 844-6458
www.acraretail.org

American Conference of Academic Deans
1818 R Street NW
Washington, DC 20009
(202) 884-7419
www.acad-edu.org

American Council for Construction Education
1717 North Loop 1604 East, Suite 320
San Antonio, TX 78232-1570
(210) 495-6161
www.acce-hq.org

American Council of Trustees and Alumni
1726 M Street NW, Suite 802
Washington, DC 20036-4525
(202) 467-6787
www.goacta.org

American Council of Education
One Dupont Circle NW
Washington, DC 20036
(202) 939-9300
www.acenet.edu

American Counseling Association
5999 Stevenson Ave.
Alexandria, VA 22304
(800) 347-6647
www.counseling.org/

American Culinary Federation Foundation Accrediting Commission
180 Center Place Way
St. Augustine, FL 32095
(904) 824-4468
www.acfchefs.org

American Education Research Association
1430 K Street, NW, Suite 1200
Washington, DC 20005
(202) 238-3200
http://www.aera.net/

American Forensic Association
Box 256
River Falls, WI 54022-0256
(715) 425-9533
www.americanforensics.org

American Institute of Architecture Students
1735 New York Avenue, NW
Washington, DC 20006-5209
(202) 626-7472
www.aias.org

American Psychological Association
750 First Street NE
Washington, DC 20002-4242
(800) 374-2721 or (202) 336-5500
www.apa.org/

American Society for Engineering Education
1818 N Street, N.W., Suite 600
Washington, DC 20036-2479
(202) 331-3500
www.asee.org/

American Society for Training and Development
1640 King Street
Alexandria, VA 22313-1443
(800) 628-2783 or (703) 683.8100
www.astd.org/

American Society of Landscape Architects
Landscape Architectural Accreditation Board
636 Eye Street, NW
Washington, DC 20001-3736
(202) 898-2444
www.asla.org

American Student Government Association
412 NW 16th Avenue
Gainesville, FL 32601-4203
(877) 275-2742
www.asgaonline.com

APPA (Leadership in Educational Facilities)
1643 Prince Street
Alexandria, VA 22314-2818
(703) 684-1446
www.appa.org

Association for Childhood Education International
17904 Georgia Ave, Suite 215
Olney, MD 20832
(301) 570-2111 or (800) 423-3563
acei.org/

Association for Consortium Leadership
4900 Powhatan Avenue
Norfolk, VA 23529-0293
(757) 683-3183
www.acl.odu.edu

Association for Continuing Higher Education
Oklahoma Center for Continuing Education
1700 Asp Avenue
Norman, OK 73072-6400
(800) 807-2243 or (405) 329-0249
www.acheinc.org/

Association for Counselor Education and Supervision
5999 Stevenson Avenue
Alexandria, VA 22304
(866) 815-2237 or (703) 212-2237
www.acesonline.net/

Association for General and Liberal Studies
English Department, Ball State University RB 2109
Muncie, IN 47306-0460
(765) 285-8406
www.agls.org

Association for Institutional Research
1435 E Piedmont Drive, Suite 211
Tallahassee, FL 32308
(850) 385-4155
www.airweb.org

Association for International Practical Training
10400 Little Patuxent Parkway, Suite 250
Columbia, MD 21044-3519
(410) 997-2200
www.aipt.org

Association for Prevention Teaching and Research
1001 Connecticut Avenue NW, Suite 610
Washington, DC 20036
(202) 463-0550
www.aptrweb.org

Association for Supervision and Curriculum Development
1703 North Beauregard St.,
Alexandria, VA 22311-1714
(800) 933-2723
www.ascd.org

Association for the Study of Higher Education
University of Nevada Las Vegas
Box 453068 - 4505 S. Maryland Parkway
Las Vegas NV 89154-3068
(702) 895-2737
www.ashe.ws

Association of American Colleges and Universities
1818 R Street NW
Washington, DC 20009
(202) 387-3760
www.aacu.org

Association of American Universities
1200 New York Ave, NW, Suite 550
Washington, DC 20005
(202) 408-7500
www.aau.edu

Association of Teacher Educators
8505 Euclid Ave., Suite 3
Manassas Park, VA 20111-2407
(703) 331-0911
www.ate1.org/pubs/home.cfm

Association of American University Presses
28 West 36th Street, Suite 602
New York, NY 20018
(212) 989-1010
www.aaupnet.org

Association of Catholic Colleges and Universities
One Dupont Circle, Suite 650
Washington, DC 20036
(202) 457-0650
www.accunet.org

Association of College and University Housing Officers-International
941 Chatham Lane, Suite 318
Columbus, OH 43221-2416
(614) 292-0099
www.acuho-i.org

Association of College Unions International
One City Centre, Suite 200
120 W. Seventh St.
Bloomington, IN 47404
(812) 245-2284
www.acui.org

Association of Collegiate Business Schools and Programs
11520 West 119th Street
Overland Park, KS 66213
(913) 339-9356
www.acbsp.org

Association of Collegiate Conference and Events Directors-International
419 Canyon Ave. Suite 311
Fort Collins, CO 80521
(970) 449-4960
www.acced-i.org

Association of Collegiate Schools of Architecture
1735 New York Avenue, NW
Washington, DC 20006
(202) 785-2324
www.acsa-arch.org

Association of Collegiate Schools of Planning
6311 Mallard Trace
Tallahassee, FL 32312
(850) 385-2054
www.acsp.org

Association of Community College Trustees
1233 20th Street NW, Suite 301
Washington, DC 20036
(202) 775-4667
www.acct.org

The Association of Educational Publishers
300 Martin Luther King Blvd., Ste. 200
Wilmington, DE 19801
(302) 295-8350
www.aepweb.org

Association of Governing Boards of Universities and Colleges
1133 20th Street NW, Suite 300
Washington, DC 20036
(202) 296-8400
www.agb.org

Association of Graduate Liberal Studies Programs
c/o Duke University, Box 90095
Durham, NC 27708-0095
(919) 684-1987
www.aglsp.org

Association of Jesuit Colleges and Universities
One Dupont Circle, Suite 405
Washington, DC 20036
(202) 862-9893
www.ajcunet.edu

Association of Military Colleges and Schools of the United States
3604 Glenbrook Road
Fairfax, VA 22031
(703) 272-8406
www.amcsus.org

The Association of Public and Land-Grant Universities
(formerly National Association of State Universities and Land-Grant Colleges)
1307 New York Avenue, N.W., Suite 400
Washington, DC 20005-4722
(202) 478-6040
http://www.aplu.org/

Association of Specialized and Professional Accreditors
1020 West Byron Street, Suite 8G
Chicago, IL 60613-2987
(773) 857-7900
www.aspa-usa.org

Association of Teacher Education
P.O. Box 793
Manassas, VA 20113
(703) 331-0911
www.ate1.org

Association of University Research Parks
6262 N. Swan Road, Suite 100
Tucson, AZ 85718
(520) 529-2521
www.aurp.net

Association of University Summer Sessions
University of Arizona
PO Box 210066, Room 221
Tucson, AZ 85721-0066
(520) 626-8488
outreach.olemiss.edu/auss/

Career College Association
1101 Connecticut Ave. NW, Suite 900
Washington, DC 20036
(202) 336-6700
www.career.org

The Carnegie Foundation for the Advancement of Teaching
51 Vista Lane
Stanford, CA 94305
(650) 566-5100
www.carnegiefoundation.org

Center for Women Policy Studies
1776 Massachusetts Avenue, NW Suite 450
Washington, DC 20036
(202) 872-1770
www.centerwomenpolicy.org

Center on Education and Training for Employment
The Ohio State University
College of Education and Human Ecology
1900 Kenny Road
Columbus, OH 43210-1016
(614) 292-8008
www.cete.org

The College Board
45 Columbus Avenue
New York, NY 10023-6917
(212) 713-8000
www.collegeboard.com

Columbia Scholastic Press Association
Columbia University, Mail Code 5711
New York, NY 10027-6902
(212) 854-9400
cspa.columbia.edu/

Commission on Independent Colleges and Universities in New York
17 Elk Street, PO Box 7289
Albany, NY 12224
(518) 436-4781
www.cicu.org

Committee on Institutional Cooperation
1819 South Neil Street, Suite D
Champaign, IL 61820-7271
(217) 333-8475
www.cic.net

Council for Adult and Experiential Learning
55 East Monroe Street, Suite 1930
Chicago, IL 60603
(312) 499-2600
www.cael.org

Council for Advancement and Support of Education
1307 New York Avenue NW, Suite 1000
Washington, DC 20005-4701
(202) 328-2273
www.case.org

Council for Aid to Education
215 Lexington Avenue - 21st Floor
New York, NY 10016-6023
(212) 661-5800
www.cae.org

Council for Exceptional Children
2900 Crystal Drive, Suite 1000
Arlington, VA 22202-3557
(888) 232-7733
www.cec.sped.org/

Council for Higher Education Accreditation
One Dupont Circle NW, Suite 510
Washington, DC 20036
(202) 955-6126
www.chea.org

Council for International Exchange of Scholars
1400 K Street, NW, Suite 700
Washington, DC 20005
(202) 686-4000
www.cies.org

Council for the Advancement of Standards in Higher Education
One Dupont Circle NW, Suite 300
Washington, DC 20036-1188
(202) 862-1400
www.cas.edu

Council of Graduate Schools
One Dupont Circle NW, Suite 230
Washington, DC 20036
(202) 223-3791
www.cgsnet.org

Council of Independent Colleges
One Dupont Circle NW, Suite 320
Washington, DC 20036
(202) 466-7230
www.cic.edu

Council on Governmental Relations
1200 New York Ave NW, Suite 750
Washington, DC 20005
(202) 289-6655
www.cogr.edu

Council on Law in Higher Education
9386 Via Classico West
Wellington, FL 33411
(561) 792-4440
www.clhe.org

Council on Occupational Education
7840 Roswell Road
Building 300, Suite 325
Atlanta, GA 30350
(770) 396-3898
www.council.org

Council on Undergraduate Research
734 15th Street, Suite 550
Washington, DC 20005
(202) 783-4810
www.cur.org

Distance Education and Training Council
1601 Eighteenth Street, NW
Washington, DC 20009
(202) 234-5100
www.detc.org

Education Commission of the States
700 Broadway, Suite 810
Denver, CO 80203
(303) 299-3600
www.ecs.org

Education Development Center, Inc.
43 Foundry Avenue
Waltham, MA 02453-8313
(617) 969-7100
www.edc.org

Friends Association for Higher Education
1501 Cherry Street
Philadelphia, PA 19102
(215) 241-7116
www.earlham.edu/~fahe/

The George Washington University HEATH Resource Center
Graduate School of Education and Human Development
2134 G Street, NW
Washington, DC 20052
(202) 994-8860
www.heath.gwu.edu/

Higher Education Resource Services
University of Denver, The Chambers Center
1901 E. Asbury Avenue
Denver, CO 80208-1002
(303) 871-6866
www.hersnet.org/

The Higher Learning Commission of the North Central Association of Colleges and Schools
230 South LaSalle Street, Suite 7-500
Chicago, IL 60604
(800) 621-7440 or (312) 263-0456
www.ncahlc.org/

International Association of Campus Law Enforcement Administrators
342 N. Main Street
West Hartford, CT 06117-2507
(860) 586-7517
www.iaclea.org/

The Institute for Higher Education Policy
1320 19th Street, NW, Suite 400
Washington, DC 20036
(202) 861-8223
www.ihep.org/

Institute of International Education
809 United Nations Plaza
New York, NY 10017
www.iie.org/

International Association of Baptist Colleges and Universities
8120 Sawyer Brown Road, Suite 108
Nashville, TN 37221-1410
(615) 673-1896
www.baptistschools.org/

International Council on Education for Teaching
National-Louis University
1000 Capitol Drive
Wheeling, IL 60090
(847) 947-5881
icet4u.org/

International Reading Association
800 Barksdale Rd., PO Box 8139
Newark, DE 19714-8139
(800) 336-7323 for U.S. and Canada or (302) 731-1600
www.reading.org/

Journalism Association of Community Colleges
PO Box 163509
Sacramento, CA 95816
www.jacconline.org/

LASPAU: Academic and Professional Programs for the Americas
25 Mount Auburn Street
Cambridge, MA 02138-6095
(617) 495-5255
www.laspau.harvard.edu/

Law School Admissions Council
662 Penn Street, Box 40
Newtown, PA 18940
(215) 968-1001
www.lsac.org/

Liaison Committee on Medical Education Association of American Medical Colleges
2450 N Street, N.W.
Washington, DC 20037
(202) 828-0596
www.lcme.org/ and http://www.aamc.org/

Lutheran Educational Conference of Northern America
2601 S Minnesota Ave., Suite 105
Box #377
Sioux Falls, SD 57105-4750
(605) 271-9894
www.lutherancolleges.org/

Middle States Commission on Higher Education
3624 Market Street
Philadelphia, PA 19104
(267) 284–5000
www.msche.org/

Midwest Association of Colleges and Employers
1255 SW Prairie Trail Parkway
Ankeny, IA 50023-7068
(515) 244-6515
www.mwace.org/

Midwestern Higher Education Compact
1300 South Second St. Suite 130
Minneapolis, MN 55454-1079
(612) 626-8288
www.mhec.org/

NACAS: National Association of College Auxiliary Services
3 Boar's Head Lane
Charlottesville, VA 22903-4610
(434) 245-8425
www.nacas.org/

NAFSA: Association of International Educators
1307 New York Avenue, NW, 8th Floor
Washington, DC 20005-4701
(202) 737.3699
www.nafsa.org/

National Association of Student Personnel Administrators
(now Student Affairs Administrators in Higher Education)
111 K Street, NE, 10th Floor
Washington, DC 20002
(202) 265-7500
www.naspa.org/

National Academic Advising Association
Kansas State University
2323 Anderson Avenue, Suite 225
Manhattan, KS 66502-2912
(785) 532-5717
www.nacada.ksu.edu/

National Academy of Education
500 Fifth Street, NW
Washington, DC 20001
(202) 334-2341
www.naeducation.org/

National Accrediting Commission of Cosmetology Arts and Sciences
4401 Ford Ave. Suite 1300
Alexandria, VA 22302
(703) 600-7600
www.naccas.org/

National Association for Bilingual Education
8701 Georgia Avenue
Silver Spring, MD 20910
www.nabe.org

National Association for College Admission Counseling
1050 N Highland Street, Suite 400
Arlington, VA 22201
(800) 822-6285
www.nacacnet.org/

National Association for Equal Opportunity in Higher Education
209 Third Street, SE
Washington, DC 20003
(202) 552-3300
www.nafeo.org/

National Association for Kinesiology & Physical Education in Higher Education
William Paterson University, Dept. of Exercise and Movement Sciences
300 Pompton Rd.
Wayne, NJ 07470
(973) 720-2419
www.nakpehe.org/index.html

National Association for Legal Support of Alternative Schools
PO Box 2823
Santa Fe, NM 87504
(505) 474-0300
www.nalsas.org/

National Association of Agricultural Educators
300 Garrigus Building, University of Kentucky
Lexington, KY 40546-0215
(800) 509-0204 or (859) 257-2224
www.naae.org/

National Association of College Stores
500 E. Lorain St.
Oberlin, OH 44074
(800) 622-7498
www.nacs.org/

National Association of College and University Attorneys
One Dupont Circle, Suite 620
Washington, DC 20036
(202) 833-8390
www.nacua.org/

National Association of College and University Business Officers
1110 Vermont Avenue, NW, Suite 800
Washington, DC 20005
(202) 861-2500
www.nacubo.org/

The National Association of College and University Food Services
2525 Jolly Road, Suite 280
Okemos, MI 48864-3680
(517) 332-2494
www.nacufs.org/

National Association of Colleges and Employers
62 Highland Ave.
Bethlehem, PA 18017
(800) 544-5272 or (610) 868-1421
www.naceweb.org/

National Association of Educational Procurement
5523 Research Park Drive, Suite 340
Baltimore, MD 21228
(443) 543-5540
www.naepnet.org/

National Association of Independent Colleges and Universities
1025 Connecticut Ave., NW, Suite 700
Washington, DC 20036
(202) 785-8866
www.naicu.edu/

National Association of State Directors of Teacher Education and Certification
1225 Providence Road, PMB #116
Whitinsville, MA 01588
(508) 380-1202
www.nasdtec.org/

National Association of State Universities and Land-Grant Colleges
(now The Association of Public and Land-Grant Universities)
1307 New York Avenue, NW, Suite 400
Washington, DC 20005-4722
(202) 478-6040
www.aplu.org/

National Association of Student Financial Aid Administrators
1101 Connecticut Avenue, NW, Suite 1100
Washington, DC 20036-4303
(202) 785-0453
www.nasfaa.org/

National Association of Student Personnel Administrators
(now Student Affairs Administrators in Higher Education)
111 K Street, NE, 10th Floor
Washington, DC 20002
(202) 265-7500
www.naspa.org/

National Association of System Heads
1250 H St NW, Suite 700
Washington, DC 20005
(202) 887-0614
www.nashonline.org/

National Catholic Educational Association
1005 North Glebe Road, Suite 525
Arlington, VA 22201
(800) 711-6232
www.ncea.org/

National Coalition for Campus Children's Centers
950 Glenn Drive, Suite 150
Folsom, CA 95630
(877) 736-6222
www.campuschildren.org

National Commission for Cooperative Education
360 Huntington Avenue, 384 CP
Boston, MA 02115-5096
(617) 373-3770
www.co-op.edu/

National Council for Accreditation of Teacher Education
2010 Massachusetts Ave NW, Suite 500
Washington, DC 20036
(202) 466-7496
www.ncate.org/

National Council for Continuing Education and Training
PO Box 820062
Portland, OR 97282-1062
(503) 233-1842
www.nccet.org/

National Council for the Social Studies
8555 Sixteenth Street, Suite 500
Silver Spring, MD 20910
(301) 588-1800
www.socialstudies.org/

National Council of Instructional Administrators
Department of Educational Administration
141 Teachers College Hall, PO Box 880360
University of Nebraska-Lincoln
Lincoln, NE 68588-0360
(402) 472-3727
www.nciaonline.org/

National Council of Teachers of Mathematics
1906 Association Drive
Reston, VA 20191-1502
(800) 235-7566 or (703) 620-9840
www.nctm.org/

National Council of University Research Administrators
1225 19th Street, NW, Suite 850
Washington, DC 20036
(202) 466-3894
www.ncura.edu/content/

National Commission on Adult and Experiential Learning
104 Johnson Street
Marshall, TX, 75670
(903) 935-3890

National Council on Economic Education
122 East 42nd Street, Suite 2600
New York, NY 10168
(212) 730-7007 or (800) 338-1192
www.councilforeconed.org/

National Council on Measurement in Education
2424 American Lane
Madison, WI 53704
(608) 443-2487
www.ncme.org/

National Education Association
1201 16th Street, NW
Washington, DC 20036-3290
(202) 833-4000
www.nea.org/

National Reading Conference
7044 S.13th St.
Oak Creek, WI 53154
(414) 908-4924
www.nrconline.org/

National Rural Education Association
Purdue University
100 N. University St.
West Lafayette, IN 47907
(765) 494-0086
www.nrea.net/

National Safety Council College and University Initiative
1121 Spring Lake Drive
Itasca, IL 60143-3201
(800) 621-7615
www.nsc.org/

National Science Teachers Association
1840 Wilson Boulevard
Arlington, VA 22201
(703) 243-7100
www.nsta.org/

National Society for Experiential Education
19 Mantua Road, Mt.
Royal, NJ 08061
(856) 423-3427
www.nsee.org/

National Writing Project
University of California
2105 Bancroft Way #1042
Berkeley, CA 94720-1042
(510) 642-0963
www.nwp.org/

New England Association of Schools and Colleges, Inc.
Commission on Institutions of Higher Education
209 Burlington Rd, Suite 201
Bedford, MA 01730-1433
(781) 271-0022
cihe.neasc.org/

New England Association of Schools and Colleges, Inc.
Commission on Technical and Career Institutions
209 Burlington Rd, Suite 201
Bedford, MA 01730-1433
(781) 271-0022
ctci.neasc.org/

New England Board of Higher Education
45 Temple Place
Boston, MA 02111
(617) 357-9620
www.nebhe.org/

North America Association of Summer Sessions
Division of Continuing Education and Professional Development
Bradley University, 1501 W. Bradley Ave.
Peoria, IL 61625
naass.org/

North Central Association Commission on Accreditation and School Improvement
Arizona State University
P.O. Box 871008
Tempe, AZ 85287-1008
(800) 525-9517
www.ncacasi.org/

North Central Conference on Summer Sessions
nccss.org/

Northwest Commission on Colleges and Universities
8060 165th Avenue NE, Suite 100
Redmond, WA 98052
(425) 558- 4224
www.nwccu.org/

Pennsylvania Association of Colleges and Universities
Suite 15 No. 214, 950 Walnut Bottom Rd
Carlisle, PA 17015
(800) 687-9010
www.pacu.org/

Quality Education for Minorities (QEM) Network
1818 N Street, NW, Suite 350
Washington, DC 20036
(202) 659-1818
www.qem.org/

Society for College and University Planning
1330 Eisenhower Place
Ann Arbor, MI 48108
(734) 764-2000
www.scup.org/

Society for History Education
(562) 985-2573
www.thehistoryteacher.org/

Society for Nutrition Education
9100 Purdue Road, Suite 200
Indianapolis, IN 46268
(317) 328-4627 or (800) 235-6690
www.sne.org/

Society for Public Health Education
10 G Street, NE, Suite 605
Washington, DC 20002
(202) 408-9804
www.sophe.org/

Society for Values in Higher Education
PO Box 751-SVHE c\o Portland State University
Portland, OR 97207-0751
(503) 725-2575
www.svhe.org/

Southern Universities Research Association
1201 New York Ave. NW, Suite 430
Washington, DC 20005
(202) 408.7872
www.sura.org/home/index.html

Southern Association for College Student Affairs
Armstrong Atlantic State University
11935 Abercorn Street
Savannah, GA 31419
(912) 344-2510
www.sacsa.org/

Southern Association of Colleges and Schools Commission on Colleges
1866 Southern Lane
Decatur, GA 30033
(404) 679-4500
www.sacscoc.org/

Southern Regional Education Board
592 10th St. NW
Atlanta, GA 30318-5776
(404) 875-9211
www.sreb.org/

Student Affairs Administrators in Higher Education
(formerly National Association of Student Personnel Administrators)
111 K Street, NE, 10th Floor
Washington, DC 20002
(202) 265-7500
www.naspa.org/

State Higher Education Executive Officers
3035 Center Green Drive, Suite 100
Boulder, CO 80301-2205
(303) 541-1600
www.sheeo.org/

Tennessee Independent Colleges and Universities Association
1031 17th Avenue South
Nashville, TN 37212
(615) 242.6400
www.ticua.org/

Transitional Association of Christian Colleges and Schools
P.O. Box 328
Forest, VA 24551
(434) 525-9539
www.tracs.org/

United Negro College Fund
8260 Willow Oaks Corporate Drive
P.O. Box 10444
Fairfax, VA 22031-8044
(800) 331-2244
www.uncf.org/

University Continuing Education Association
One Dupont Circle, Suite 615
Washington, DC 20036
(202) 659-3130
connect.upcea.edu/

University Cultural Center Association
3939 Woodward Ave Suite 100
Detroit, MI 48201
(313) 420-6000
detroitmidtown.com/05/

Urban Affairs Association
University of Wisconsin-Milwaukee
P.O. Box 413
Milwaukee, WI 53201-0413
(414) 229-3025
urbanaffairsassociation.org/

Western Association of Schools and Colleges Accrediting Commission for Community and Junior Colleges
10 Commercial Blvd, Ste 204
Novato, CA 94949
(415) 506-0234
www.accjc.org/

Western Association of Schools and Colleges Accrediting Commission for Schools
533 Airport Boulevard, Suite 200
Burlingame, CA 94010-2009
(650) 696-1060
www.acswasc.org/

Western Association of Schools and Colleges Accrediting Commission for Senior Colleges and Universities
985 Atlantic Avenue, Suite 100
Alameda, CA 94501
(510) 748-9001
www.wascsenior.org/

Western Interstate Commission for Higher Education
3035 Center Green Drive, Suite 200
Boulder, CO 80301-2204
(303) 541-0200
www.wiche.edu/

Women in Higher Education
5376 Farmco Drive
Madison, WI 53704
(608) 251-3232
www.wihe.com/

HEALTH & RECREATION

Accreditation Council for Pharmacy Education
135 S. LaSalle Street, Suite 4100
Chicago, IL 60603-4810
Phone: (312) 664-3575
www.acpe-accredit.org

Accrediting Bureau of Health Education Schools
7777 Leesburg Pike, Suite 314 N
Falls Church, VA 22043
(703) 917-9503
www.abhes.org

American Academy of Kinesiology and Physical Education
P.O. Box 5076
Champaign, IL 61825-5076
www.aakpe.org

American Alliance for Health, Physical Education, Recreation & Dance
1900 Association Dr.
Reston, VA 20191-1598
(703) 476-3400
www.aahperd.org/

American Association for Leisure and Recreation
1900 Association Drive
Reston, VA 20191-1599
(800) 213-7193 or (703) 476-3400
www.aahperd.org/

American Association of Blood Banks Committee on Accreditation of Specialist in Blood Banking Technology Schools
8101 Glenbrook Road
Bethesda, MD 20814-2749
(301) 907-6977
www.aabb.org

American Association of Colleges of Nursing
One Dupont Circle, NW, Suite 530
Washington, DC 20036
(202) 463-6930
www.aacn.nche.edu

American Association of Colleges of Osteopathic Medicine
5550 Friendship Blvd., Suite 310
Chevy Chase, MD 20815-7231
(301) 968-4101
www.aacom.org

American Association of Medical Assistants
20 N. Wacker Dr., Ste. 1575
Chicago, IL 60606
(312) 899-1500
www.aama-ntl.org

American Association of Nurse Anesthetists
Council on Accreditation of Nurse Anesthesia Educational Programs
222 S. Prospect Avenue
Park Ridge, IL 60068
(847) 692-7050
www.aana.com

American College of Nurse-Midwives
8403 Colesville Rd, Suite 1550
Silver Spring, MD 20910
(240) 485-1800
www.midwife.org

American Dental Association Commission on Dental Accreditation
211 East Chicago Ave.
Chicago, IL 60611-2678
(312) 440-2500
www.ada.org/117.aspx

American Dietetic Association
120 South Riverside Plaza, Suite 2000
Chicago, IL 60606-6995
(800) 877-1600 or (312) 899-0040
www.eatright.org/

American Nurses Association
8515 Georgia Avenue, Suite 400
Silver Spring, MD 20910-3492
(301) 628-5000
www.nursingworld.org/

American Optometric Association
Accreditation Council on Optometric Education
243 N. Lindbergh Blvd.
St. Louis, MO 63141
(800) 365-2219
www.theacoe.org

American Osteopathic Association
142 E. Ontario St.
Chicago, IL 60611
(800) 621-1773
www.aoacoca.org

American Physical Therapy Association
1111 North Fairfax Street
Alexandria, VA 22314-1488
(703) 684-APTA (2782) or (800) 999-2782
www.apta.org

American Public Health Association
800 I Street, NW
Washington, DC 20001-3710
(202) 777-2742
www.apha.org/

American Speech-Language Hearing Association
2200 Research Boulevard
Rockville, MD 20850-3289
(301) 296-5700
www.asha.org/

Association for the Advancement of Health Education
1900 Association Dr.
Reston, VA 20191-1598
(703) 476-3400 or (800) 213-7193
www.aahperd.org/

Association of American Medical Colleges
2450 N Street, NW
Washington, DC 20037-1126
(202) 828-0400
www.aamc.org

Association of Schools of Allied Health Professions
4400 Jenifer Street, NW, Suite 333
Washington, DC 20015
(202) 237-6481
www.asahp.org/

Association of University Programs in Health Administration
2000 14th Street North, Suite 780
Arlington, VA 22201
(703) 894-0940
www.aupha.org

Commission on Accreditation for Health Informatics and Information Management Education
233 N. Michigan Avenue, 21st Floor
Chicago, IL 60601-5800
(312) 233-1100
www.cahiim.org

Commission on Accreditation of Allied Health Education Programs
1361 Park Street
Clearwater, FL 33756
(727) 210-2350
www.caahep.org

Commission on Accreditation of Healthcare Management Education
2111 Wilson Boulevard, Suite 700
Arlington, VA 22201
(703) 351-5010
www.cahme.org

Commission on Accreditation of Rehabilitation Facilities
6951 E. Southpoint Road
Tucson, AZ 85756
(520) 325-1044 or (888) 281-6531
www.carf.org

Commission on Opticianry Accreditation
One Dupont Circle NW, Suite 510
Washington, DC 20036-1135
(202) 955-6126
www.coaccreditation.org

Council of Colleges of Acupuncture and Oriental Medicine
600 Wyndhurst Avenue, Suite 112
Baltimore, MD 21210
(410) 464-6040
www.ccaom.org

Council on Aviation Accreditation
Aviation Accreditation Board International
3410 Skyway Drive
Auburn, AL 36830
(334) 844-2431
www.aabi.aero

Council on Chiropractic Education Commission on Accreditation
8049 North 85th Way
Scottsdale, AZ 85258-4321
(480) 443-8877
www.cce-usa.org

Council on Education for Public Health
800 Eye Street NW, Suite 202
Washington, DC 20001-3710
(202) 789-1050
www.ceph.org

Council on Naturopathic Medical Education
PO Box 178
Great Barrington, MA 01230
(413) 528-8877
www.cnme.org

Council on Podiatric Medical Education
9312 Old Georgetown Road
Bethesda, MD 20814-1621
(301) 581-9200
www.cpme.org

Council on Social Work Education
1701 Duke Street, Suite 200
Alexandria, VA 22314
(703) 683-8080
www.cswe.org/

Liaison Committee on Medical Education
2450 N Street, NW
Washington, DC 20037
(202) 828-0596
www.lcme.org/

National Accreditation Council for Agencies Serving People with Blindness or Visual Impairment
7017 Pearl Rd.
Middleburg Hts., OH 44130
(440) 545-1601
www.nacasb.org/

National Association for Practical Nurse Education and Service, Inc.
1940 Duke Street, Suite 200
Alexandria, VA 22314
(703) 933-1003
www.napnes.org/

National Association for Sport and Physical Education
1900 Association Drive
Reston, VA 20191
(703) 476-3410 or (800) 213-7193
www.aahperd.org/naspe/

National Association of Advisors for the Health Professions
P.O. Box 1518
Champaign, IL 61824-1518
(217) 355-0063
www.naahp.org/

The National Association of College and University Food Services
2525 Jolly Road, Suite 280
Okemos, MI 48864-3680
(517) 332-2494
www.nacufs.org/

The National Athletic Trainers Association
2952 Stemmons Freeway #200
Dallas, TX 75247
(214) 637-6282
www.nata.org/

National Coalition for Campus Children's Centers
University of Northern Iowa, PLS #114E
Cedar Falls, IA 50614-3593
(800) 813-8207 or (319) 273-3113
www.campuschildren.org

National Collegiate Athletic Association
950 Glenn Drive Suite 150
Folsom, CA 95630
(877) 736-6222
www.ncaa.org/

National League for Nursing
61 Broadway, 33rd Floor
New York, NY 10006
(212) 363-5555
www.nln.org/

Society for Nutrition Education
9100 Purdue Road, Suite 200
Indianapolis, IN 46268
(317) 328-4627 or (800) 235-6690
www.sne.org/

Society for Public Health Education
10 G Street, NE, Suite 605
Washington, DC 20002
(202) 408-9804
www.sophe.org/

University Aviation Association
3410 Skyway Drive
Auburn, AL 36830-6444
(334) 844-2434
www.uaa.aero/

HISTORY, ETHNIC & CULTURAL HISTORIES

African Studies Association
54 Joyce Kimer Ave
Piscataway, NJ 08854
(848) 445-8173
www.africanstudies.org/

American Association for State and Local History
1717 Church Street
Nashville, TN 37203-2991
(615) 320-3203
www.aaslh.org/

American Historical Association
400 A Street SE
Washington, DC 20003-3889
(202) 544-2422
www.historians.org/

American Oriental Society
Hatcher Graduate Library, University of Michigan
Ann Arbor, MI 48109-1205
(734) 647-4760
www.umich.edu/~aos/

American Society for Ethnohistory
Department of History, York University
2140 Vari Hall, 4700 Keele Street
Toronto, Ontario, Canada, M3J 1P3
(416) 736-5123, ext. 66960
www.ethnohistory.org/

American Studies Association
1120 19th Street NW, Suite 301
Washington, DC 20036
(202) 467-4783
www.theasa.net/

Association for Asian Studies, Inc.
825 Victors Way, Suite 310
Ann Arbor, MI 48108
(734) 665-2490
www.asian-studies.org/

The Association for Canadian Studies in the United States
2030 M Street, NW, Suite 350
Washington, DC 20036
(202) 775-9007
www.acsus.org/

Association for Jewish Studies
15 West 16th Street
New York, NY 10011
(917) 606-8249
www.ajsnet.org/

The Association for the Study of African American Life and History
Howard Center, 2225 Georgia Avenue, NW, Suite 331
Washington, DC 20059
(202) 238-5910
www.asalh.org/

Community Colleges Humanities Association
c/o Essex County College, 303 University Avenue
Newark, NJ 07102
(973) 877-3577
www.ccha-assoc.org/

Economic History Association
Department of Economics, 500 El Camino Real
Santa Clara University
Santa Clara, CA 95053-0385
(408) 554-4348
www.eh.net/eha/

International Studies Association
324 Social Sciences Building
University of Arizona
Tucson, AZ 85721
(520) 477-2050
www.isanet.org/

Latin American Studies Association
416 Bellefield Hall
University of Pittsburgh
Pittsburgh, PA 15260
(412) 648-7929
lasa.international.pitt.edu/

Middle East Studies Association of North America
1219 N. Santa Rita Avenue
The University of Arizona
Tucson, AZ 85721
(520) 621-5850
www.mesa.arizona.edu/

National Association for Ethnic Studies, Inc.
Western Washington University
995 East Green Street #519
Pasadena, CA 91106-2410
(970) 491-3927
www.ethnicstudies.org/

National Council for Black Studies
National Office, P.O. Box 4109
Atlanta, GA 30302-4109
(513) 556-0785
www.ncbsonline.org/

Organization of American Historians
112 Bryan Street
Bloomington, IN 47408
(812) 855-7311
www.oah.org/

Society for Slovene Studies
University of Washington
Suzzallo Library, Box 352900
Seattle, WA 98195
(206) 543-5588
www.arts.ualberta.ca/~ljubljan/

Society for the Advancement of Scandinavian Study
HRCB, Brigham Young University
Provo, UT 84602-6118
(801) 422-5598
www.scandinavianstudy.org/

LANGUAGES, LITERATURE & WRITING

American Association for Applied Linguistics
PMB 321 2900 Delk Rd, Ste 700
Marietta, GA 30067-5350
(866) 821-7700
www.aaal.org/

American Association of Teachers of Arabic
3416 Primm Lane
Birmingham, AL 35216
(205) 822-6800
aataweb.org/

American Association of Teachers of French
Southern Illinois University
Carbondale, IL 62901
(618) 453-5731
www.frenchteachers.org/

American Association of Teachers of German
112 Haddontowne Court, #104
Cherry Hill, NJ 08034-3668
(856) 795-5553
www.aatg.org/

American Association of Teachers of Italian
Indiana University
Department of French and Italian
Ballantine Hall 642
1020 E. Kirkwood Avenue
Bloomington, IN 47405-6601
www.aati-online.org/

American Association of Teachers of Slavic and East European Languages
AATSEEL, P.O. Box 569
Beloit, WI 53512-0569
(608) 361-9697
www.aatseel.org/

American Association of Teachers of Spanish and Portuguese
900 Ladd Road
Walled Lake, MI 48390
(248) 960-2180
www.aatsp.org/

American Classical League
Miami University of Ohio
Oxford, OH 45056
(513) 529-7741
www.aclclassics.org/

American Comparative Literature Association
University of Texas at Austin
1 University Station B5003
Austin, TX 78712-0196
(803) 777-3021
www.acla.org/

American Council of Teachers of Russian
ACTR is a Division of American Councils for International Education
1828 L Street N.W., Suite 1200
Washington, DC 20036
(202) 833-7522
membership.actr.org/

American Philological Association
University of Pennsylvania
220 S. 40th St., Suite 201E
Philadelphia, PA 19104-3512
(215) 898-4975
www.apaclassics.org/

American Translators Association
225 Reinekers Lane, Suite 590
Alexandria, VA 22314
(703) 683-6100
www.atanet.org/

Associated Writing Programs
George Mason University; MS 1E3
Fairfax, VA 22030-4444
(703) 993-4301
www.awpwriter.org/

Association of Departments of English
26 Broadway, 3rd floor
New York, NY 10004-1789
(646) 576-5130
www.ade.org

Association of Departments of Foreign Languages
26 Broadway, 3rd floor
New York, NY 10004-1789
(646) 576-5140
www.adfl.org

Association of Teachers of Japanese
240 Humanities Bldg., 279 UCB
Boulder, CO 80309-0279
(303) 492-5487
www.aatj.org/atj/

Association of Teachers of Technical Writing
PO Box 793
Manassas, VA 20113
(940) 565-4458
www.attw.org

Chinese Language Teachers Association
Department of Foreign Language & Literature
University of Wisconsin-Milwaukee, P.O Box 413
Milwaukee, WI 53201
clta-us.org/

College English Association
English Dept., MSC 1801, James Madison University
Harrisonburg, VA 22807
(716) 649-7900
www.cea-web.org/index.php

Community Colleges Humanities Association
Essex County College, 303 University Avenue
Newark, NJ 07102
(973) 877-3577
www.ccha-assoc.org/

Conference on College Composition and Communication
1111 W. Kenyon Road
Urbana, IL 61801-1096
(217) 328-3870 or (877) 369-6283
www.ncte.org/cccc

The Council of Writing Program Administrators
312 Lake Ontario Hall, Grand Valley State University
Allendale, MI 49401
(734) 487-4220
www.wpacouncil.org

Journalism Association of Community Colleges
PO Box 163509
Sacramento, CA 95816
www.jacconline.org/

Linguistic Society of America
1325 18th St. NW #211
Washington, DC 20036-6501
(202) 835-1714
www.lsadc.org/

Modern Language Association of America
26 Broadway, 3rd floor
New York, NY 10004-1789
(646) 576-5000
www.mla.org/

National Council of Teachers of English
1111 W. Kenyon Road
Urbana, IL 61801-1096
(217) 328-3870 or (877) 369-6283
www.ncte.org/

National Writing Project
www.nwp.org/

Teachers of English to Speakers of Other Languages
1925 Ballenger Avenue, Suite 550
Alexandria, Virginia 22314-6820
(703) 836-0774 or toll free (888) 547-3369
www.tesol.org

LIBRARIES & MUSEUMS

Association of African-American Museums
P.O. Box 427
Wilberforce, OH 45384
(937) 352-5084
www.blackmuseums.org/

The American Association of Law Libraries
105 W. Adams Street, Suite 3300
Chicago, IL 60603
(312) 939-4764
www.aallnet.org/

American Association of Museums
1575 Eye Street NW Suite 400
Washington, DC 20005
(202) 289-1818
www.aam-us.org/

American Institute for Conservation of Historic and Artistic Works
9719 Natalies Way
Ellicott City, MD 21042
(410) 905-2777
www.museumsusa.org/

American Library Association
50 E. Huron
Chicago, IL 60611
(800) 545-2433
www.ala.org/

American Library Association Office for Accreditation
50 E. Huron St.
Chicago, IL 60611
(312) 280-2432
www.ala.org/accreditation

American Society for Information Science
1320 Fenwick Lane, Suite 510
Silver Spring, MD 20910
(301) 495-0900
www.asis.org/

American Theological Library Association
300 South Wacker Drive, Suite 2100
Chicago, IL 60606-6701
(888) 665-2852
www.atla.com/

Art Libraries Society of North America
(800) 817-0621
www.arlisna.org/

Association for Library and Information Science Education
65 E Wacker Place, Suite 1900
Chicago, IL 60601-7246
(312) 795-0996
www.alise.org

Association of College and Research Libraries
50 E. Huron
Chicago IL 60611
(800) 545-2433
www.ala.org/ala/mgrps/divs/acrl/index.cfm

Association of Research Libraries
21 Dupont Circle NW, Suite 800
Washington, DC 20036
(202) 296-2296
www.arl.org

Music Library Association
8551 Research Way, Suite 180
Middleton, WI 53562
(608) 836-5825
musiclibraryassoc.org/

Society of American Archivists
17 North State Street, Suite 1425
Chicago, IL 60602
(312) 606-0722 or toll-free (866) 722-7858
www2.archivists.org/

Special Libraries Association
331 South Patrick Street
Alexandria, VA 22314-3501
(703) 647-4900
www.sla.org/

MATHEMATICS, TECHNOLOGY & BUSINESS

AACSB: The International Association for Management Education
AACSB International
777 South Harbour Island Boulevard, Suite 750
Tampa, FL 33602-5730
(813) 769-6500
www.aacsb.edu/

ABET, Inc.
111 Market Place, Suite 1050
Baltimore, MD 2102
(410) 347-7700
www.abet.org

ACUTA: The Association for Information Communications Technology Professionals in Higher Education
152 West Zandale Drive, Suite 200
Lexington, KY 40503-2486
(859) 278-3268
www.acuta.org

Academy of Legal Studies in Business
Miami University, Department of Finance
120 Upham Hall
Oxford, OH 45056
(800) 523-8180
www.alsb.org

Accrediting Commission of Career Schools and Colleges of Technology
2101 Wilson Boulevard, Suite 302
Arlington, VA 22201
(703) 247-4212
www.accsct.org

Association for the Advancement of Artificial Intelligence
2275 East Bayshore Road, Suite 160
Palo Alto, California 94303
(650) 328-3123
www.aaai.org/

American Economic Association
2014 Broadway, Suite 305
Nashville, TN 37203-2418
(615) 322-2595
www.vanderbilt.edu/AEA/

American Mathematical Society
201 Charles Street
Providence, RI 02904-2294
(401) 455-4000 or (800) 321-4267
www.ams.org/

American Mathematical Association of Two Year Colleges
Southwest Tennessee Community College
5983 Macon Cove
Memphis, TN 38134
(901) 333-6243
www.amatyc.org

American Society for Engineering Education
1818 N Street NW, Suite 501
Washington, DC 20036-2479
(202) 331-3500
www.asee.org/

American Society for Engineering Education and Technology
1320 Fenwick Lane, Suite 410
Silver Spring, MD 20910
(301) 495-0900
www.asis.org/

American Statistical Association
732 North Washington Street
Alexandria, VA 22314-1943
(703) 684-1221
www.amstat.org

Association for Business Communication
PO Box 6143
Nacogdoches, TX 75962-6143
(936) 468-6280
www.businesscommunication.org

Association for Business Simulation and Experiential Learning
Arcadia University, Dept. of Bus/Health Admin. & Economics
450 S. Easton Road
Glenside, PA 19038
(215) 572-2849
www.absel.org

Association for Career and Technical Education
(formerly American Vocational Association)
1410 King Street
Alexandria, VA 22314
(800) 826-9972
www.acteonline.org

Association for Computational Linguistics
209 N Eighth Street
Stroudsburg, PA 18360
(570) 476-8006
www.aclweb.org/

Association of Technology, Management, and Applied Engineering
(formerly National Association of Industrial Technology)
1390 Eisenhower Place
Ann Arbor, MI 48108
(734) 677-0720
www.atmae.org/

CSAB, Inc. – Computing Sciences Accreditation Board
817 Loyola Dr.
Towson, MD 21204
(410) 339-5456
www.csab.org/

Decision Sciences Institute
Georgia State University
J. Mack Robinson College of Business
University Plaza
Atlanta, GA 30303
(404) 413-7710
www.decisionsciences.org/

Direct Marketing Association, Inc.
1120 Avenue of the Americas
New York, NY 10036-6700
(212) 768-7277
www.the-dma.org/index.php

Direct Marketing Educational Foundation, Inc.
1120 Avenue of the Americas
New York, NY 10036-6700
(212) 768-7277
www.directworks.org/

EDUCAUSE
1150 18th Street NW, Suite 1010
Washington, DC 20036-3816
(202) 872-4200
www.educause.edu

Financial Management Association International
University of South Florida, College of Business Administration
4202 East Fowler Avenue, BSN 3331
Tampa, FL 33620-5500
(813) 974-2084
www.fma.org/

International Assembly for Collegiate Business Education
PO Box 3960
Olathe, KS 66063
(913) 631-3009
www.iacbe.org/

Mathematical Association of America
1529 18th St. NW
Washington, DC 20036-1358
(202) 387-5200 or (800) 741-9415
www.maa.org

National Association of College and University Business Officers
1110 Vermont Avenue, NW, Suite 800
Washington, DC 20005
(202) 861-2500
www.nacubo.org/

National Association of Industrial Technology
(now the Association of Technology, Management, and Applied Engineering)
1390 Eisenhower Place
Ann Arbor, MI 48108
(734) 677-0720
atmae.org/

National Business Education Association
1914 Association Drive
Reston, VA 20191
(703) 860-8300
www.nbea.org/

National Council on Economic Education
122 East 42nd Street, Suite 2600
New York, NY 10168
(212) 730-7007 or (800) 338-1192
www.councilforeconed.org/

National Council of Teachers of Mathematics
1906 Association Drive
Reston, VA 20191-1502
(800) 235-7566 or (703) 620-9840
www.nctm.org/

Organizational Systems Research Association
Morehead State University, Department of Information Systems
150 University Boulevard, Box 2478
Morehead, KY 40351-1689
(606) 783-2718
www.osra.org/

PHILOSOPHY & RELIGION

American Academy of Religion
825 Houston Mill Rd NE STE 300
Atlanta, GA 30329-4205
(404) 727-3049
www.aarweb.org/

American Catholic Philosophical Association
University of St. Thomas
3800 Montrose Blvd.
Houston, TX 77006
(713) 942-3483
www.acpaweb.org

The American Philosophical Association
University of Delaware, 31 Amstel Avenue
Newark, DE 19716-4797
(302) 831-1112
www.apaonline.org

The American Philosophical Society
105 South Fifth Street
Philadelphia, PA 19106-3387
(215) 440-3400
www.amphilsoc.org/

Association for Biblical Higher Education
5575 S. Semoran Boulevard, Suite 26
Orlando, FL 32822-1781
(407) 207-0808
www.abhe.org

Association for Clinical Pastoral Education, Inc.
1549 Clairmont Road, Suite 103
Decatur, GA 30033
(404) 320-1472
www.acpe.edu

Association for College and University Religious Affairs
Macalester College, Center for Religious and Spiritual Life
1600 Grand Avenue
St. Paul, MN 55105
(651) 696-6293
www.site.acuraonline.net/

Association of Catholic Colleges and Universities
One Dupont Circle, Suite 650
Washington, DC 20036
(202) 457-0650
www.accunet.org

Association of Practical Theology
Princeton Theological Seminary
Tennent Hall, 108 Stockton Street
Princeton, NJ 08540
(609) 477-7739
www.practicaltheology.org

Association of Presbyterian Colleges and Universities
100 Witherspoon Street
Louisville, KY 40202
(502) 569-5364 or (888) 728-7228 ext. 5364
www.presbyteriancolleges.org

Association of Theological Schools in the United States and Canada
The Commission on Accrediting
10 Summit Park Drive
Pittsburgh, PA 15275-1110
(412) 788-6505
www.ats.edu

Council for Christian Colleges and Universities
321 Eighth Street NE
Washington, DC 20002
(202) 546-8713
www.cccu.org

Council of Societies for the Study of Religion
Rice University - MS156, PO Box 1892
Houston, TX 77251-1892
(713) 348-5721
www.cssr.org

Society of Biblical Literature
The Luce Center, 825 Houston Mill Road
Atlanta, GA 30329
(404) 727-3100
www.sbl-site.org/

United States Conference of Catholic Bishops Commission on Certification and Accreditation
3211 South Lake Drive, Suite #317
St. Francis, WI 53235-3702
(414) 486-0139
www.usccbcca.org/

SCIENCES

American Academy of Microbiology Committee on Postgraduate Educational Programs
1752 N Street NW
Washington, DC 20036-2804
(202) 942-9225
www.asm.org/cpep

American Association for Clinical Chemistry
1850 K St. NW, Suite 625
Washington, DC 20006-2215
(800) 892-1400 or (202) 857-0717
www.aacc.org/

American Association for the Advancement of Science
1200 New York Avenue NW
Washington, DC 20005
(202) 326-6400
www.aaas.org/

American Association of Anatomists
9650 Rockville Pike
Bethesda, MD 20814-3998
(301) 634-7910
www.anatomy.org/

American Association of Physics Teachers
One Physics Ellipse
College Park, MD 20740-3845
(301) 209-3311
www.aapt.org/

American Astronomical Society
2000 Florida Ave., NW, Suite 400
Washington, DC 20009-1231
(202) 328-2010
aas.org/

American Chemical Society
1155 Sixteenth Street, NW
Washington, DC 20036
(800) 227-5558 (US) or (202) 872-4600 (Worldwide)
acs.org/

American Chemical Society Committee on Professional Training
1155 Sixteenth Street NW
Washington, DC 20036
(202) 872-4600
www.acs.org/cpt

American Geological Institute
4220 King Street
Alexandria, VA 22302-1502
(703) 379-2480
www.agiweb.org/

American Institute of Biological Sciences
1444 I St., NW, Ste. 200
Washington, DC 20005
(202) 628-1500
www.aibs.org/

American Institute of Physics
One Physics Ellipse
College Park, MD 20740-3843
(301) 209-3100
www.aip.org/

American Physical Society
One Physics Ellipse,
College Park, MD 20740-3844
(301) 209-3200
www.aps.org/

American Physiological Society
9650 Rockville Pike
Bethesda, MD 20814-3991
(301) 634-7164
www.the-aps.org/

American Society for Biochemistry and Molecular Biology
11200 Rockville Pike, Suite 302
Rockville, MD 20852-3110
(240) 283-6600
www.asbmb.org/

American Society for Cell Biology
8120 Woodmont Avenue, Suite 750
Bethesda, MD 20814-2762
(301) 347-9300
www.ascb.org/

American Society for Horticultural Science
1018 Duke Street
Alexandria, VA 22314
(703) 836-4606
www.ashs.org/

American Society for Microbiology
1752 N Street, NW
Washington, DC 20036-2904
(202) 737-3600
www.asm.org/

American Society of Cytopathology
www.cytopathology.org

American Veterinary Medical Association
1931 North Meacham Road, Suite 100
Schaumburg, IL 60173-4360
(800) 248-2862
www.avma.org

Botanical Society of America
PO Box 299
St. Louis, MO 63166-0299
(314) 577-9566
www.botany.org/

Council for Agricultural Sciences and Technology
4420 West Lincoln Way
Ames, IA 50014-3447
(515) 292-2125
www.cast-science.org

Council of Colleges of Arts and Sciences
The College of William and Mary
P.O. Box 8795
Williamsburg, VA 23187-8795
(757) 221-1784
www.ccas.net

Ecological Society of America
1990 M Street, NW, Suite 700
Washington, DC 20036
(202) 833-8773
www.esa.org/

Entomological Society of America
www.entsoc.org/

Geological Society of America
P.O. Box 9140
Boulder, CO 80301-9140
(303) 357-1000
www.geosociety.org/

National Accrediting Agency for Clinical Laboratory Sciences
5600 N. River Rd., Suite 720
Rosemont, IL 60018-5119
(847) 939-3597 and (773) 714-8880
www.naacls.org/

National Forensic Association
http://www.nationalforensics.org/about

National Science Teachers Association
1840 Wilson Boulevard
Arlington VA 22201
(703) 243-7100
www.nsta.org/

Society of American Foresters
5400 Grosvenor Lane
Bethesda, MD 20814-2198
(301) 897-8720
www.safnet.org/

SOCIAL SCIENCES

Academy of Political Science
Political Science Quarterly
475 Riverside Drive, Suite 1274
New York, NY 10115-1274
(212) 870-2500
www.psqonline.org/

American Anthropological Association
2200 Wilson Blvd., Suite 600
Arlington, VA 22201
(703) 528-1902
www.aaanet.org/

American Bar Association
321 North Clark Street
Chicago, IL 60654-7598
(312) 988-5000
www.abanet.org

American Geographical Society
32 Court Street, Suite 201
Brooklyn, New York 11201-4404
(718) 624-2212
www.amergeog.org/

American Political Science Association
1527 New Hampshire Ave, NW
Washington, DC 20036-1206
(202) 483-2512
www.apsanet.org/

American Psychological Association
Office of Program Consultation and Accreditation
750 First Street, NE
Washington, DC 20002-4242
(202) 336-5979
www.apa.org/ed/accreditation

The American Real Estate & Urban Economics Association
The Florida State University - College of Business
821 Academic Way, 248 RBB
Tallahassee, FL 32306-1110
(866) 273-8321
www.areuea.org

American Sociological Association
1430 K Street, NW Suite 600
Washington, DC 20005
(202) 383-9005
www.asanet.org/

Archaeological Institute of America
Boston University
656 Beacon Street, 6th Floor
Boston, MA 02215-2006
(617) 353-9361
www.archaeological.org/

Association of American Geographers
1710 16th Street, NW
Washington, DC 20009-3198
(202) 234-1450
www.aag.org/

Association of American Law Schools
1201 Connecticut Avenue NW, Suite 800
Washington, DC 20036-2717
(202) 296-8851
www.aals.org

Gerontological Society of America
1220 L Street NW, Suite 901
Washington, DC 20005
(202) 842-1275
www.geron.org/

PhD Planner

PhD Planner Contents

1	**Monthly Academic Planner** Because mapping your year is a good idea
2	**A Four Year Plan** Long term planning for courses
3	**Planning for Comprehensive Exams and Thesis Proposals** The trials and tribulations of a doc student
4	**Academic Job Search Budget** Manage your dough
5	**Inventory of Professional Readiness** Progress check
6	**Institutional Fit Inventory** If the shoe fits…
7	**Creating and Using a Support Network** I get by with a little help from my friends
8	**Letters of Recommendation** Who can speak to my potential as a scholar?
9	**Transcripts** Evidence of degree attainment
10	**Marketing Tools** My scholarly proof
11	**Letter and Application Log** Staying on top of your applications
12	**Teaching Philosophy Inventory** Knowing your stuff as a teacher

PhD Planner Contents

13	**Teaching Philosophy Profile** My beliefs on teaching and learning in the academy
14	**Teaching Agenda** In a perfect world, I'd teach...
15	**Research Inventory** Because knowing your research matters
16	**Research Profile** My beliefs on research in my field
17	**Portfolio Checklist** Showcasing my goods
18	**Employer Profile** Advanced interview homework
19	**On-Campus Visit** Advanced interview preparation
20	**Interview Notes** The basic questions you have to nail
21	**Apparel and Packing Planner** Looking good was never this easy
22	**Community Inventory** Can I live here?
23	**Academic Negotiations** There's more to this than salary Part 1
24	**Academic Negotiations** There's more to this than salary Part 2
25	**My Thank You List** A little thanks goes a long way

I

PhD Planner

MONTHLY ACADEMIC PLANNER

KEY DATES AND ACTION

August:	
September:	
October:	
November:	
December:	
January:	

PhD Planner

MONTHLY ACADEMIC PLANNER

KEY DATES AND ACTION

February:	
March:	
April:	
May:	
June:	
July:	

2 PhD Planner

A FOUR YEAR PLAN

LONG TERM PLANNING FOR COURSEWORK

Year 1:

Year 2:

Year 3:

Year 4:

Practica Placements/Internships:

PhD Planner 3

PLANNING FOR COMPREHENSIVE EXAMS/THESIS PROPOSAL

KEY DATES AND DETAILS

Comprehensive Exam Format/Date:
Proposal Date:

Major Areas of Study/Emphasis:

Key Notes:

Committee members (potential or confirmed)/Thesis/Comps

List name and title and specialty area

-
-
-
-
-

Chair of Committee (potential or confirmed)

-

4 PhD Planner

ACADEMIC JOB SEARCH BUDGET

MANAGE YOUR DOUGH

Budget items	Estimated cost	Actual cost
Expenses during job seeking		
Pre-interview Expenses		
CV materials/preparation		
Transcripts		
Interfolio		
Attire • Suit • Tie/scarf • Shirt/Blouse • Shoes		
Interview Expenses (perhaps reimbursed) • Transportation • Hotel • Food • Misc.		
Basic Expenses		
Tuition and associated fees (books, technology)		
Housing/living (rent, mortgage, groceries, utilities)		
Transportation (car, public transport, travel)		
Additional bills (credit card, college loans)		
Childcare/Healthcare		
Other		

PhD Planner 5

INVENTORY OF PROFESSIONAL READINESS

PROGRESS CHECK

✓	**Professional Identity** Career goals Active research agenda (present; publish) Involvement (campus; professional) Networking	Notes:
✓	**Marketing Strategies** CV Cover letter ePortfolio Samples of work Letters of recommendation	Notes:
✓	**Interview Readiness** Job resources Interview questions Philosophy statements Job talk Teaching demonstration Professional presence	Notes:
✓	**Employment Considerations** Type of institution (mission, colleagues, students, size, location, ranking) Professional development (tenure, teaching, research, service) Right fit/right place Compensation Appointment details	Notes:

6 PhD Planner

INSTITUTIONAL FIT INVENTORY

IF THE SHOE FITS. . .

Institutional Mission

Are you interested in a campus with a research or teaching emphasis; 2 year or 4 year; undergraduate or graduate programs?

Institutional Size/Type

Are you interested in a public or private, large or small, international or regional, religious, independent campus? How is the institution funded?

Strategic Plans, Vision, Mission

What are the goals of the institution?

Faculty & Student Demographic Profile

Where do students come from? Where do they go after graduation? Is the population diverse?

Key Faculty Responsibilities

Are you a teacher? Researcher? Both?

Department size/type

What kind of colleagues do you want?

Student population

Are you interested in working with graduate students, undergraduates, international, non-traditional, online? Part-time/full-time students?

Position type

Are you looking for a tenure-track, clinical, adjunct, part-time, online, 9 or 12 month, administrative or professional-type position? Institutions may offer various types of jobs.

PhD Planner

7

CREATING AND USING A SUPPORT NETWORK

"I GET BY WITH A LITTLE HELP FROM MY FRIENDS" THE BEATLES

Mentor

University Advisor

Supervisors

Former students

Peers (TAs, GAs)

Parents/partners

8 PhD Planner

LETTERS OF RECOMMENDATION

WHO CAN SPEAK TO MY POTENTIAL AS A SCHOLAR?

NAME/TITLE: RELATIONSHIP TO ME:	
EMAIL:	PHONE:
ADDRESS:	
THEIR STRENGTHS AS A REFERENCE:	

NAME/TITLE: RELATIONSHIP TO ME:	
EMAIL:	PHONE:
ADDRESS:	
THEIR STRENGTHS AS A REFERENCE:	

NAME/TITLE: RELATIONSHIP TO ME:	
EMAIL:	PHONE:
ADDRESS:	
THEIR STRENGTHS AS A REFERENCE:	

PhD Planner

8

LETTERS OF RECOMMENDATION

WHO CAN SPEAK TO MY POTENTIAL AS A SCHOLAR?

NAME/TITLE: RELATIONSHIP TO ME:	
EMAIL:	PHONE:
ADDRESS:	
THEIR STRENGTHS AS A REFERENCE:	
NAME/TITLE: RELATIONSHIP TO ME:	
EMAIL:	PHONE:
ADDRESS:	
THEIR STRENGTHS AS A REFERENCE:	
NAME/TITLE: RELATIONSHIP TO ME:	
EMAIL:	PHONE:
ADDRESS:	
THEIR STRENGTHS AS A REFERENCE:	

9 PhD Planner

TRANSCRIPTS

EVIDENCE OF DEGREE ATTAINMENT

Undergraduate Degree:

REGISTRAR:

EMAIL:

PHONE:

WEBSITE:

Master's Degree:

REGISTRAR:

EMAIL:

PHONE:

WEBSITE:

Master's Degree:

REGISTRAR:

EMAIL:

PHONE:

WEBSITE:

PhD Degree:

REGISTRAR:

EMAIL:

PHONE:

WEBSITE:

International Certificates/Study:

REGISTRAR:

EMAIL:

PHONE:

WEBSITE:

PhD Planner 10

MARKETING TOOLS

SCHOLARLY PROOF

CV draft: Saved and backed up at: Date: Proofed:
Cover letter draft: Saved and backed up at: Date: Proofed:
Teaching philosophy draft: Saved and backed up at: Date:
Research statement draft: Saved and backed up at: Date:
Syllabi: Teaching materials: Saved and backed up at: Date:

Additional Materials:

PhD Planner

LETTER & APPLICATION LOG

KEEPING TRACK OF YOUR APPLICATIONS

Job title:
Institution:
Date applied:
Key points:

Job title:
Institution:
Date applied:
Key points:

Job title:
Institution:
Date applied:
Key points:

Job title:
Institution:
Date applied:
Key points:

Notes:

PhD Planner 12

TEACHING PHILOSOPHY INVENTORY

BECAUSE BRAINSTORMING MAKES IT EASIER

I dig the following theories of learning:

How I use formative assessment:

How I assess student learning:

My grading scheme:

How I reflect/encourage/value diversity in my teaching:

How I address different learning styles:

How I integrate technologies:

Do I offer support outside of class:

Some unique learning strategies I use:

13 PhD Planner

TEACHING PHILOSOPHY PROFILE

MY BELIEFS ON TEACHING AND LEARNING IN THE ACADEMY

Why am I a good teacher?

What would others say about my teaching (students, supervisors)?

What do I believe about the process of teaching and learning (3 statements)?

1.
2.
3.

What are three examples of my philosophy in action from my teaching?

1.
2.
3.

What are three examples of my philosophy in action with students outside the classroom? Advising? Mentoring?

1.
2.
3.

PhD Planner

14

TEACHING AGENDA

IN A PERFECT WORLD I'D TEACH...

What introductory courses would you teach?

1.
2.
3.

What advance level courses would you teach?

1.
2.
3.

What specialized seminars would you teach?

1.
2.

What courses would you like to develop?

1.
2.

How would you deliver these courses? Are you open to teaching online?

How I integrate technologies:

Do I offer support outside of class:

15 PhD Planner

RESEARCH INVENTORY

BECAUSE BRAINSTORMING MAKES IT EASIER

What is my research area/specialty?

My theoretical and methodological approach is:

I use the following quantitative and qualitative methods:

I use the following technologies (statistical programs, medical devices, lab equipment):

Lab protocols include:

The following ethical principles guide my work:

The following sources provide external support in my area:

How do I involve undergraduate and graduate students?

My future research goals include:

PhD Planner 16

RESEARCH PROFILE

MY BELIEFS ON RESEARCH IN MY FIELD

Why am I a good researcher?

What would others say about my research potential, my specialty?

What are my current research projects?

1.
2.
3.

What are my future research interests?

1.
2.
3.

In five years I plan to have…

1.
2.
3.

17 PhD Planner

PORTFOLIO CHECKLIST

SHOWCASING MY GOODS

✓	**Credentials** Degrees Licenses/Certificates Scholarships/Fellowships Internships/Externships/Practica	Notes:
✓	**Teaching** Teaching Experiences/Assistantships Philosophy/Agenda Syllabi Evaluations Awards Demonstration Videos	Notes:
✓	**Research** Research Experiences/Assistantships Posters/Papers/Presentations Statement/Agenda Dissertation Abstract/Writing Sample Publications Honors & Awards	Notes:
✓	**Service** Agenda/Statement Professional Service Leadership	Notes:

PhD Planner 18

EMPLOYER PROFILE

ADVANCE INTERVIEW HOMEWORK

Enrollment & Student Success Rates

undergraduate; graduate; commuters

retention/drop-out rates; post-secondary majors; internship opportunities

Strategic Plans, Vision, Mission

5-10 year plans for institution, department, vision and mission statements

Faculty & Student Demographic Profile

race; ethnic origins; religion; linguistic background; family composition

Key Faculty

area of expertise; publications; grants

Institution/Department Strengths

What is their brand? Reputation? Stellar programs/departments

Placement Rates

jobs within field; unemployment rate; type of employers

Accreditation & Affiliation

state, regional, national agencies; religious, single gender colleges, historically black colleges and universities, specific populations or curricular focus

Aid Allotment & Endowment

federal loans; state aid; campus work-study; campus grants

major donors; future plans

19 PhD Planner

ON-CAMPUS VISIT

ADVANCE INTERVIEW PREPARATION

Name of institution:
Primary contact:
Address:
Email:
Cell:

Travel arrangements:
Flight:
Departure:
Arrival:
Who's meeting me? Name/title:

Hotel:
Name:
Phone:

Special functions/dinners/activities:
#1 Function:
Host:
Time and place:

#2 Function:
Host:
Time and place:

#3 Function:
Host:
Time and place:

#4 Function:
Host:
Time and place:

PhD Planner 20

INTERVIEW NOTES

THE BASIC QUESTIONS YOU HAVE TO NAIL

Why this position is of interest to me:

A bit about myself:

Why I am a unique candidate:

Main essence of my teaching philosophy:

My research interests:

My view of collaboration:

My service agenda:

Courses I can teach now; in the future:

Grants and funding initiatives:

Publications in process:

21 PhD Planner

APPAREL & PACKING PLANNER

LOOKING GOOD WAS NEVER THIS EASY

Travel outfit:

First day of interviews:

Evening attire (first night):

Second day of interviews:

Evening attire (second night):

Accessories:

	One small travel bag		extra cash
	cell phone/iPad/iPod & chargers		umbrella
	overcoat		flash drive
	laptop		copies of handouts/CVs
	professional dress shoes		mints/protein bars

Other:

PhD Planner 22

COMMUNITY INVENTORY

CAN I LIVE HERE?

✓	**Community Profile** Geographic area & features Climate & weather Urban/suburban/rural/international Demographic info Schools & institutions of learning Community services	Notes:
✓	**Socio-economic profile** Educational attainment Major employers Unemployment rate Crime statistics Growth rate Demographic statistics & projections	Notes:
✓	**Recreation & Personal Interest** Sports & sports facilities Fine arts venues Cultural scene Nightlife Children friendly activities Religion	Notes:
✓	**Housing** Home type: single family, condo, etc. Housing cost & availability Density	Notes:

23 PhD Planner

ACADEMIC NEGOTIATIONS

THERE'S MORE TO THIS THAN SALARY

Negotiables	✓	Priority notes:
Appointment title (classification, rank)		
Start date		
Salary (starting)		
Salary (options: consulting, bonuses, extra assignments; joint appointments)		
Teaching load		
Number of course releases (any time constraints?)		
Summer teaching/support opportunities		
Teaching duties (selection of courses; materials; class size; interdisciplinary opportunities)		
Advising responsibilities		
Tenure process; tenure clock; tenure status		
Facilities/office/lab space		
Technology resources/support		
Research/lab equipment		

PhD Planner

24

ACADEMIC NEGOTIATIONS

THERE'S MORE TO THIS THAN SALARY

Negotiables	✓	Priority notes:
Grant support/grant expectations		
Travel budget & general budget (conferences, pd, supplies, journal memberships)		
Graduate assistants		
Staff support (secretarial and administrative)		
Immigration and Visa/Green Card Sponsor (legal assistance and fees for obtaining necessary visas)		
Relocation support (moving expenses, temporary housing, community connections)		
Campus facilities (parking, recreational, library, athletics, and office/teaching/research facilities)		
Benefits (healthcare insurance, retirement, vacation and sick leave, parental leave)		
Opportunities for significant other/partner/spousal hires		
Tuition benefits for dependents		
Childcare		

25 PhD Planner

MY THANK YOU LIST

A LITTLE THANKS GOES A LONG WAY

Mentors & Advisors

Reference Writers

Supervisors

New Colleagues

Peers (TAs, GAs)

Parents/partners

Notes

Made in the USA
San Bernardino, CA
21 August 2015